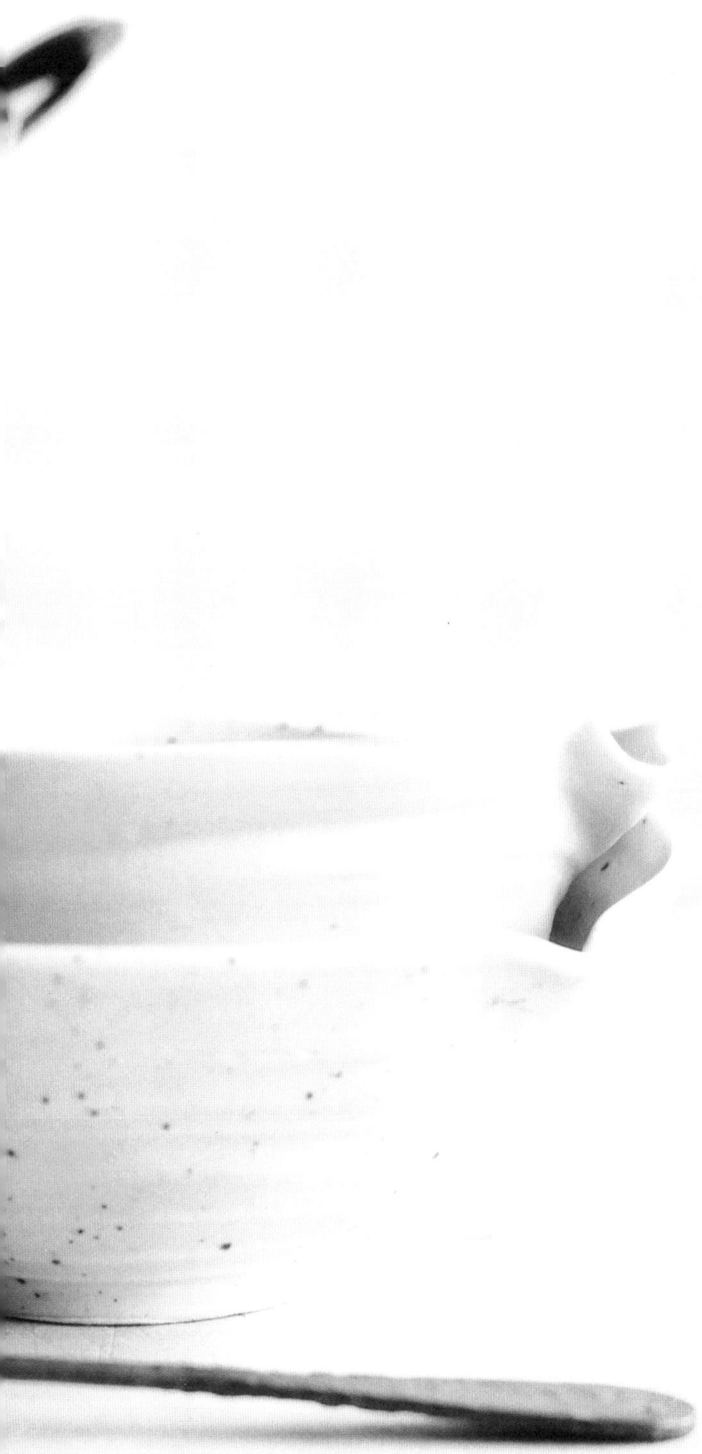

The
Fast Five
shortcuts to deliciousness

Photography by Chris Court + Con Poulos

THE FAST FIVE
Copyright © Donna Hay Pty Ltd 2022
Design copyright © Donna Hay Pty Ltd 2022
Photography copyright © Chris Court and Con Poulos 2022
Recipes and styling: Donna Hay
Art direction and design: Chi Lam
Art director and managing editor: Hannah Schubert
Copy editor: Mariam Digges
Recipe testing: Jacinta Cannataci and Tina McLeish
dh Sponsorships and collaborations manager: Rebecca Jones
dh Digital strategist and producer: Lauren Gibb

Fourth Estate
An imprint of HarperCollins*Publishers*

HarperCollins*Publishers*
Australia • Brazil • Canada • France • Germany • Holland • India
Italy • Japan • Mexico • New Zealand • Poland • Spain • Sweden
Switzerland • United Kingdom • United States of America

First published in Australia in 2022
by HarperCollins*Publishers* Australia Pty Limited
Level 13, 201 Elizabeth Street, Sydney NSW 2000
ABN 36 009 913 517
harpercollins.com.au

A catalogue record for this book is available from the National Library of Australia
ISBN 978 1 4607 6287 5

On the cover: ceramic plates and vintage forks by Chris Court

Reproduction by Hannah Schubert and Splitting Image
Printed and bound in China by RR Donnelley on 140gsm Golden Sun Woodfree
6 5 4 3 2 1   22 23 24 25 26

donna hay

The
Fast Five
shortcuts to deliciousness

FOURTH ESTATE

Contents

Savoury

Sweet

I know how easy it is to get stuck on the same weekly repertoire of recipes – that safety net of dishes we know by heart. *The Fast Five* features your all-time favourites, reimagined as five instant flavour hits, thanks to my tasty shortcuts and 'why didn't I think of that?' switch-ups.

These recipes still live in that comfort zone of reassuring deliciousness, but with more personality, crunch and punchy flavour than ever!

With a simple change-up, weeknight dinners transform into flavour-forward crowd-pleasers. If I can add a burst of freshness and some pantry magic into a crumb, filling or patty, you can enjoy all your take-out favourites in super yum, better-for-you ways – and faster than it takes to order in!

You'll also find my ready-in-a-flash desserts – soaked in all the sticky, nostalgic dreaminess that always fills the house with amazing scents – but with five fast, nice-for-you twists.

Look out for the QR codes along the way that you can scan and bring the pages to life with instant videos featuring my clever tips and flavour tricks.

This is the ultimate collection of time-saving, upflavoured riffs on the classics; I'm sure they will become your new family favourites. Enjoy!

Savoury

Spaghetti

A pantry forage, ingredient makeover and burst of freshness rewards you with bright, flavour-forward pastas like you've never seen! Coated in silky sauces and starring plenty of punch, cream and greens, these tasty, twirlable bowls are ready in minutes.

silky parmesan pasta with crispy crumb

400g dried spaghetti
1 cup (250ml) pure cream
4 egg yolks, lightly beaten
1 cup (80g) finely grated parmesan, plus extra to serve
sea salt and cracked black pepper
4 cups (100g) wild leaf rocket (arugula), chopped, plus extra
   to serve
2 teaspoons finely grated lemon rind
crispy crumb
2 cups (140g) fresh sourdough breadcrumbs
2 tablespoons extra virgin olive oil
2 teaspoons dried chilli flakes

To make the crispy crumb, preheat oven to 180°C (350°F). Line a large baking tray with non-stick baking paper.

Combine the breadcrumbs, oil and chilli flakes. Place on the prepared tray and bake for 5–8 minutes or until golden, stirring occasionally. Set aside.

Cook the pasta in a large saucepan of boiling salted water until al dente. Drain and set aside.

Whisk the cream, yolk and parmesan together in a bowl to combine.

Return the pan over low heat. Add the parmesan cream mixture and cook for 2 minutes, stirring gently with a spatula, until silky and slightly thickened, but not scrambled. Sprinkle with salt and pepper.

Add the pasta and cook for 1–2 minutes, stirring, until it is coated in the sauce and heated through. Stir through the rocket and rind.

Divide the pasta between serving bowls and sprinkle with the crispy crumb, the extra rocket and extra parmesan. **SERVES 4**

 SCAN TO WATCH ME
CREATE THIS RECIPE

green goddess pasta with zucchini and haloumi

300g haloumi, crumbled
2 tablespoons chopped oregano leaves
1 tablespoon extra virgin olive oil
300g dried spaghetti
3 zucchinis (courgettes), shredded using a julienne peeler
sea salt and cracked black pepper
3 cups (75g) baby spinach leaves
green goddess sauce
1 small avocado, halved and deseeded
1 cup (24g) flat-leaf parsley leaves
1 cup (16g) mint leaves
¼ cup (60ml) lemon juice
2 green onions (scallions), chopped
⅓ cup (80ml) water

TIP
Keep things dairy-free by swapping haloumi for crispy crumbs (see *recipe*, page 12).

Preheat oven grill (broiler) to high. Line a large baking tray with non-stick baking paper.

Place the haloumi and oregano on the prepared tray and drizzle with the oil. Toss to combine. Spread the haloumi out on the tray and grill for 10–12 minutes, stirring occasionally, until crisp and golden. Set aside.

To make the green goddess sauce, place the avocado, parsley, mint, lemon juice, green onion and water in a blender and blend until smooth. Set aside.

Cook the pasta in a large saucepan of boiling salted water until al dente. Drain and return the pasta to the pan.

Add the zucchini, the green goddess sauce, salt and pepper and stir through to coat. Add the spinach leaves and stir through.

Divide the pasta between serving plates and top with the crispy haloumi. **SERVES 4**

summer tomato pasta

400g dried spaghetti
800g vine-ripened heirloom tomatoes, finely chopped
½ red onion, finely chopped
1½ cups (30g) basil leaves, torn, plus extra to serve
¼ cup (60ml) extra virgin olive oil
2 tablespoons baby capers, rinsed, drained and chopped
1 tablespoon finely grated lemon rind
sea salt and cracked black pepper

TIP
When it comes to choosing your tomatoes, let the seasons guide you for the sweetest results.

Cook the pasta in a large saucepan of boiling salted water until al dente. Drain and set aside.

Place the tomatoes, red onion, basil, oil, capers, lemon rind, salt and pepper in a bowl and mix to combine. Allow to stand for 5 minutes to marinate.

Add the pasta and stir through to coat.

Divide the pasta between serving bowls. Top with the extra basil leaves, to serve. **SERVES 4**

caramelised balsamic onion pasta

2 tablespoons extra virgin olive oil

4 onions, sliced

1 tablespoon chopped tarragon leaves

sea salt and cracked black pepper

⅓ cup (80ml) balsamic vinegar

¼ cup (60ml) good-quality chicken stock

¼ cup (55g) raw caster (superfine) sugar

400g dried spaghetti

80g unsalted butter

1½ cups (150g) grated gruyère

fried sage leaves and finely grated parmesan, to serve

TIP
Fry sage leaves
in grapeseed oil
in a non-stick
frying pan over
medium-high
heat until crispy.
Drain on
absorbent
kitchen paper.

Heat a large deep frying pan over medium heat.

Add the oil, onion, tarragon, salt and pepper. Cover with a lid and cook for 10–12 minutes. Remove the lid, add the balsamic, stock and sugar and cook for 5–7 minutes or until caramelised. Set aside.

Cook the pasta in a large saucepan of boiling salted water until al dente. Drain, reserving ½ cup (125ml) of the pasta water.

Return the pasta to the pan over low heat. Add the butter, gruyère, pepper and the reserved pasta water. Stir through to coat.

Divide the pasta between serving bowls and top with the balsamic onion, fried sage leaves and parmesan. **SERVES 4**

lemon, vodka and olive martini pasta

400g dried spaghetti
¼ cup (60ml) extra virgin olive oil
4 cloves garlic, sliced
2 tablespoons baby capers, rinsed and drained
¾ cup (120g) pitted green Sicilian olives, sliced
   and ¼ cup (60ml) olive brine reserved
1½ tablespoons shredded lemon rind, plus extra to serve
¾ cup (180ml) dry vermouth
⅓ cup (80ml) vodka
1 tablespoon unsalted butter
sea salt and cracked black pepper

TIP
If you don't
have vodka,
swap it for gin.

Cook the pasta in a large saucepan of boiling salted water until
al dente. Drain and set aside.

Return the pan over medium heat. Add the oil, garlic and capers
and cook for 2 minutes or until the garlic is fragrant and starts to
colour. Add the olives and the lemon rind and cook for 1–2 minutes.
Pour in the vermouth and vodka, bring to a simmer and cook for
2 minutes.

Return the pasta to the pan and add the reserved olive brine.
Cook for 1–2 minutes. Add the butter and gently stir through
to coat.

Divide the pasta between serving plates. Sprinkle with salt and
pepper and serve with the extra lemon rind. **SERVES 4**

Bruschetta

Contrasting crunchy bread with sweet, sun-kissed vegies, a good-quality olive oil and a few heavy-lifting ingredients, these dressed-up versions of the Italian favourite make for a delicious snack, starter or side.

tomato and basil oil bruschetta

Place **2 cups (40g) basil leaves** in a heatproof bowl and cover with **boiling water**. Blanch for 10 seconds, then transfer to a **bowl of iced water** to refresh. Drain well, squeezing out excess water. Place in a blender with **½ cup (125ml) extra virgin olive oil** and **a pinch of sea salt flakes**. Blend until a bright green colour and finely chopped. Preheat char-grill pan to high. Brush **4 slices sourdough** with **extra virgin olive oil** and grill for 1 minute each side. Divide **tomato slices** between sourdough slices and drizzle with the basil oil. **SERVES 4 AS A SIDE**

caramelised garlic bruschetta

Preheat oven to 180°C (350°F). Place **1 head skin-on garlic that has been broken into cloves** and **½ cup (125ml) extra virgin olive oil** in a ramekin and cover with baking paper and aluminium foil. Bake for 30 minutes, then allow to cool slightly. Squeeze garlic into a bowl and mash together with 1 tablespoon of the garlic oil until smooth. Preheat char-grill pan to high. Brush **4 slices sourdough** with **extra virgin olive oil** and grill for 1 minute each side. Top each with **some fresh ricotta**, the mashed garlic and **some finely grated parmesan**. SERVES 4 AS A SIDE

minted zucchini bruschetta

Combine **2 grated zucchinis (courgettes)**, **2 tablespoons extra virgin olive oil, 1 tablespoon chopped mint leaves, 2 teaspoons finely grated lemon rind, sea salt and cracked black pepper**. Preheat char-grill pan to high. Brush **4 slices sourdough** with **extra virgin olive oil** and grill for 1 minute each side. Divide the minted zucchini between sourdough slices and top with **some burrata** and **dried chilli flakes**. SERVES 4 AS A SIDE

blistered tomato bruschetta

Preheat char-grill pan to high. Brush **4 slices sourdough** with **extra virgin olive oil** and grill for 1 minute each side. Preheat oven grill (broiler) to high. Combine **250g cherry tomatoes, 4 sprigs oregano, sea salt and cracked black pepper** and **a drizzle of extra virgin olive oil** on a baking tray lined with non-stick baking paper. Grill for 8–10 minutes. Divide tomatoes and oregano between sourdough slices. SERVES 4 AS A SIDE

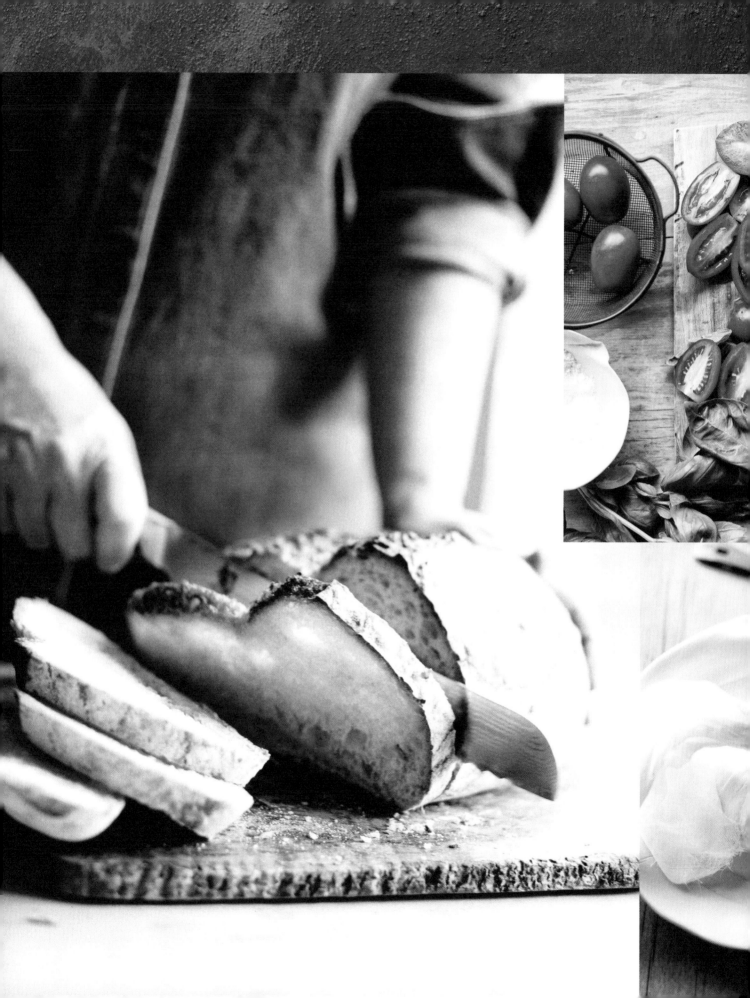

Tacos

Taco Tuesday just got a makeover! Move beyond mince and beans and load your tortillas up with these fun, fresh and fabulous flavour combinations. A spoonful of salsa and a squeeze of lime bring the zing.

cheat's chipotle chicken tacos

**1 x store-bought rotisserie chicken or 2 x cooked chicken
  breast fillets, shredded
2 chipotle chillies in adobo sauce+, chillies finely chopped
  and 2 tablespoons sauce reserved
½ white onion++, thinly sliced
250g cherry tomatoes, chopped
2 tablespoons lime juice
1 tablespoon extra virgin olive oil
sea salt and cracked black pepper
8 x 15cm (6 inch) flour tortillas, warmed
cucumber ribbons, coriander (cilantro) and smoky roasted
  chilli salsa (see *recipe,* page 39), to serve**

TIP
Use a vegetable
peeler to create
cucumber
ribbons.

Place the chicken in a bowl and add the chipotle chillies, adobo sauce,
onion, tomatoes, lime juice, oil, salt and pepper. Toss to combine.
  To assemble, divide the filling between the tortillas. Top with
cucumber ribbons, coriander and smoky roasted chilli salsa. **SERVES 4**
+ *Chipotle chilli in adobo sauce is available at most supermarkets
or at specialty stores.*
++ *White onions have a milder flavour and scent than red or
brown onions.*

spiced pork and pineapple tacos

2 teaspoons ground cumin

2 teaspoons smoked paprika

½ teaspoon ground chilli powder

sea salt and cracked black pepper

600g pork fillet, trimmed

extra virgin olive oil, for brushing

8 x 15cm (6 inch) flour tortillas, warmed

butter lettuce leaves, finely chopped fresh pineapple or
green chilli and pineapple salsa (see *recipe,* page 38),
coriander (cilantro), crumbled firm feta and thinly sliced
green chilli, to serve

TIP
Adjust the chilli
to suit your
preferred level
of heat.

Combine the cumin, paprika, chilli, salt and pepper in a shallow bowl. Add the pork fillet and roll to coat.

Heat a large non-stick frying pan over medium-high heat.

Brush the pork with oil and cook for 10–12 minutes, turning occasionally, until the pork has a deep golden crust and is cooked to your liking. Set aside for 2 minutes, then thinly slice.

To assemble, fill the tortillas with some lettuce, pineapple, coriander and sliced pork. Top with feta and green chilli. **SERVES 4**

chorizo, cauliflower and chickpea tacos

1 tablespoon extra virgin olive oil
420g chorizo (about 3), sliced
1 red onion, sliced
500g small cauliflower florets
1 x 400g can chickpeas (garbanzo beans), rinsed and drained
400g cherry tomatoes
2 teaspoons smoked paprika
1 teaspoon ground cumin
¼ cup (60ml) water
8 x 15cm (6 inch) flour tortillas, warmed
finely shredded red cabbage, coriander (cilantro) and lime and
    coriander crema (see *recipe,* page 39), to serve

TIP
My family loves a 'choose your own adventure' taco feast, where I place all the components out and let everyone build their own.

Heat a large frying pan over medium-high heat.
   Add the oil, chorizo and onion and cook, stirring occasionally, for 5 minutes or until the chorizo is golden.
   Add the cauliflower, chickpeas, tomatoes, paprika and cumin and cook for 6 minutes, stirring occasionally. Pour in the water and stir to combine. Cover the pan with a tight-fitting lid and reduce the heat to medium. Cook for 5–7 minutes or until the cauliflower is soft.
   To assemble, fill the tortillas with some cabbage and the chorizo and cauliflower mixture. Top with coriander and the lime and coriander crema. **SERVES 4**

 SCAN TO WATCH ME
CREATE THIS RECIPE

chimichurri steak tacos

600g rump steak fillets
extra virgin olive oil, for brushing
400g cherry tomatoes
8 x 15cm (6 inch) flour tortillas, warmed
shredded white cabbage and extra store-bought pickled
  jalapeños, to serve
chimichurri
½ cup (26g) finely chopped coriander (cilantro)
½ red onion, finely chopped
2 tablespoons finely chopped store-bought pickled jalapeños
1 clove garlic, finely grated
¼ cup (60ml) extra virgin olive oil
¼ cup (60ml) white wine vinegar
sea salt and cracked black pepper

TIP
For smokier
tacos, cook
the steak and
tomatoes on
the barbecue.

To make the chimichurri, combine the coriander, onion, jalapeños,
garlic, oil, vinegar, salt and pepper. Set aside.

Heat a large non-stick frying pan over high heat.

Brush the steaks with oil and sprinkle with salt and pepper. Cook
for 2–3 minutes each side or until cooked to your liking. Set aside.

Wipe the pan clean and return to medium-high heat. Add the
tomatoes and cook for 5–6 minutes or until blistered and starting
to soften.

Slice the steak into thin strips and place in a bowl. Add the
chimichurri and toss to combine.

To assemble, fill the tortillas with some cabbage, the chimichurri
steak and the tomatoes. Top with the extra jalapeños and any
remaining chimichurri. **SERVES 4**

charred corn and black bean tacos

4 corn cobs, husks pulled back
4 long green chillies, halved lengthways and deseeded
1 x 400g can black beans, rinsed and drained
1 Lebanese cucumber, chopped
½ red onion, thinly sliced
2 tablespoons lime juice
2 teaspoons finely grated lime rind
1 tablespoon extra virgin olive oil
sea salt and cracked black pepper
8 x 15cm (6 inch) flour tortillas, warmed
caramelised lime avocado salsa (see *recipe,* page 39) and
   butter lettuce leaves, to serve

TIP
To slice the corn, hold the cobs upright against a board and use a sharp knife to quickly slice downwards.

Heat a large non-stick frying pan over high heat.

Add the corn and cook for 6 minutes, turning frequently. Add the chillies and cook, turning frequently, for a further 6 minutes or until charred. Set aside to cool slightly.

Slice the corn off the cobs and place in a bowl. Add the black beans, cucumber, onion, lime juice, lime rind, oil, salt and pepper and gently toss to combine.

To assemble, spread some of the caramelised lime avocado salsa onto each tortilla. Top with some lettuce, the charred corn and black bean mixture and the charred chillies. **SERVES 4**

Salsas

Not only tasty taco toppers, these salsas make the perfect dippy accompaniment for tortilla chips, so why not make a little extra for a speedy starter?

green chilli and pineapple salsa

Combine **600g finely chopped fresh pineapple**, **1 deseeded and finely chopped Lebanese cucumber**, **1 deseeded and finely chopped long green chilli**, **2 tablespoons chopped mint leaves**, **1 tablespoon lime juice** and **sea salt flakes**.
MAKES 2 CUPS

simple tomato salsa

Combine **½ grated white onion**, **2 finely chopped tomatoes**, **2 tablespoons each of chopped coriander (cilantro) leaves and lime juice**, **1 teaspoon finely chopped red chilli**, **sea salt and cracked black pepper**. MAKES 1⅓ CUPS

caramelised lime avocado salsa

Mash **2 deseeded and chopped avocados**, **¼ grated white onion**, **2 tablespoons chopped coriander (cilantro) leaves**, **2 teaspoons finely chopped jalapeños (optional)** and **sea salt flakes together** until smooth. Heat a non-stick frying pan over high heat. Add **2 halved limes**, cut-sides down, and cook for 3–5 minutes or until charred. Squeeze **the juice from 2 charred lime halves** into the avocado mixture and combine. Serve with the **remaining charred lime**. MAKES 1½ CUPS

lime and coriander crema

Combine **1 cup (240g) sour cream**, **2 tablespoons lime juice**, **1 tablespoon finely chopped coriander (cilantro) leaves**, **1 teaspoon finely grated lime rind** and **sea salt flakes**. Sprinkle with **extra finely grated lime rind**. MAKES 1¼ CUPS

smoky roasted chilli salsa

Heat a non-stick frying pan over high heat. Brush **3 long red chillies** and **3 long green chillies** with **2 tablespoons extra virgin olive oil** and cook for 5–7 minutes or until charred and softened. Allow to cool slightly. Slice the chillies in half, remove the seeds and finely chop. Combine the chopped chillies with **2 chopped tomatoes**, **½ grated red onion**, **½ teaspoon each of finely grated garlic and smoked paprika**, **2 teaspoons red wine vinegar**, **sea salt and cracked black pepper**. MAKES 1½ CUPS

Burgers

A few surprise flavour saviours, pantry powerhouses and veg heroes fill these burgers with juicy new deliciousness. Team with a tray of crisp-on-the outside, fluffy-on-the-inside potatoes for a flipping-tasty crowd-pleaser.

beef and kimchi burger with spicy mayo

700g beef mince
1 cup (60g) panko breadcrumbs
¾ cup (210g) chopped kimchi, plus extra to serve (optional)
sea salt and cracked black pepper
4 slices cheddar cheese
6 green onions (scallions), halved
4 burger buns, halved
butter lettuce leaves, to serve
spicy mayo
½ cup (150g) whole-egg mayonnaise
1 tablespoon gochujang+ (Korean chilli paste)
1 tablespoon lime juice

TIP
If you can't find kimchi, mix a little sauerkraut with chilli sauce to make a cheat's substitute.

To make the patties, place the mince, breadcrumbs, kimchi, salt and pepper in a bowl and mix to combine. Divide the mixture into 4 patties.

Heat a large non-stick frying pan or barbecue over medium-high heat. Add the patties and cook for 4–5 minutes or until browned. Flip the patties and place a slice of cheddar on top of each. Add the green onion to the pan and cook for a further 4–5 minutes or until the patties are cooked to your liking. Remove from the pan.

While the patties are cooking, make the spicy mayo. Combine the mayonnaise, gochujang and lime juice.

To assemble, top the burger buns with lettuce, green onion, spicy mayo, the patties and extra kimchi. **SERVES 4**
+ *Find gochujang in select supermarkets and Asian grocers. If you can't find it, use any other mild chilli paste.*

maple mustard lamb and haloumi burger

700g lamb mince
1 cup (70g) fresh sourdough breadcrumbs
¼ cup (70g) Dijon mustard
2½ tablespoons pure maple syrup or honey
2 tablespoons chopped oregano leaves
sea salt and cracked black pepper
200g haloumi, thinly sliced
4 burger buns, halved
whole-egg mayonnaise, wild leaf rocket (arugula), store-bought
   pickles and salt and vinegar smashed potatoes (see *recipe*,
   page 55), to serve

TIP
I love to make
these patties
ahead of time
and freeze them
to whip out
for a speedy
midweek
dinner.

To make the patties, place the mince, breadcrumbs, mustard,
maple syrup, oregano, salt and pepper in a bowl and mix to
combine. Divide the mixture into 4 patties.

Heat a large non-stick frying pan or barbecue over medium-high
heat. Add the patties and cook for 4–5 minutes each side or until
cooked through. Remove from the pan.

Wipe the pan clean and return to the heat. Add the haloumi and
cook for 1–2 minutes each side or until golden.

To assemble, top the burger buns with the mayonnaise, rocket,
haloumi, the patties and pickles. Serve with salt and vinegar
smashed potatoes. **SERVES 4**

lemongrass pork burger

700g pork mince
1 cup (70g) fresh sourdough breadcrumbs
½ cup (26g) finely chopped coriander (cilantro) leaves
2 stalks lemongrass, white part only, finely grated
2 tablespoons finely grated ginger
1½ tablespoons fish sauce
1 tablespoon finely grated lime rind
extra virgin olive oil, for cooking
4 burger buns, halved
whole-egg mayonnaise, thinly sliced green onion (scallion),
    extra coriander (cilantro), thinly sliced long red chilli and
    lime wedges, to serve
quick pickled carrot
2 tablespoons rice wine vinegar
1 tablespoon honey
4 large carrots, peeled and shredded using a julienne peeler

TIP
If you don't
have a julienne
peeler, use
a regular
vegetable peeler
to create carrot
ribbons instead.

To make the patties, place the mince, breadcrumbs, coriander, lemongrass, ginger, fish sauce and lime rind in a bowl and mix to combine. Divide the mixture into 4 patties.

Heat a large non-stick frying pan or barbecue over medium-high heat. Add the oil and patties and cook for 4–5 minutes each side or until cooked through. Remove from the pan.

While the patties are cooking, make the quick pickled carrot. Combine the vinegar and honey in a bowl. Add the carrots and toss to combine.

To assemble, spread both sides of the burger buns with the mayonnaise. Top with the green onion, extra coriander, the patties, pickled carrot and chilli. Serve with lime wedges. **SERVES 4**

butter chicken burger

600g chicken mince

1 cup (70g) fresh sourdough breadcrumbs

⅓ cup (95g) butter chicken paste

½ cup (26g) finely chopped coriander (cilantro) leaves

1 onion, finely chopped

1 tablespoon extra virgin olive oil

warmed naan bread, cucumber ribbons+, extra mint leaves,
   store-bought mango chutney and smoky potato fries
   (see *recipe*, page 55), to serve

minted yoghurt

1 cup (250g) plain thick yoghurt

2 tablespoons finely chopped mint leaves

1 tablespoon lemon juice

TIP
Feel free to
serve these
patties in
regular burger
buns, if you like.

To make the patties, place the mince, breadcrumbs, butter chicken paste, coriander and onion in a bowl and mix to combine. Divide the mixture into 4 patties.

Heat a large non-stick frying pan or barbecue over medium-high heat. Add the patties and cook for 4–5 minutes each side or until cooked through. Remove from the pan.

While the patties are cooking, make the minted yoghurt. Combine the yoghurt, mint and lemon juice.

To assemble, top the naan bread with the minted yoghurt, cucumber ribbons, extra mint leaves, the patties and mango chutney. Serve with smoky potato fries. **SERVES 4**

+ *Create cucumber ribbons using a vegetable peeler.*

SCAN TO WATCH ME
CREATE THIS RECIPE

chipotle tofu burger

¼ cup (60g) chopped chipotle chillies in adobo sauce[+]
⅓ cup (80ml) tomato passata (purée)
2 teaspoons smoked paprika
2 tablespoons pure maple syrup
sea salt and cracked black pepper
600g firm tofu, drained and cut into 12 slices
extra virgin olive oil, for drizzling
4 burger buns, halved
mashed avocado or caramelised lime avocado salsa (see *recipe*,
    page 39), butter lettuce leaves, sliced tomato, thinly sliced
    red onion, store-bought pickled jalapeños, coriander (cilantro)
    and crunchy potato rosti (see *recipe*, page 54), to serve

TIP
Replace the tofu
with trimmed
chicken breast
fillets, if you like.

Place the chipotle chillies, passata, paprika, maple syrup, salt and
pepper in a large shallow dish. Add the tofu and turn to coat. Allow
to marinate for 10 minutes.

Preheat oven grill (broiler) to high.

Place the tofu on a baking tray lined with non-stick baking paper
and spoon the remaining marinade over. Drizzle with oil and grill for
12 minutes or until golden.

To assemble, top the burger buns with some avocado, lettuce,
tomato, the chipotle tofu, red onion, jalapeños and coriander. Serve
with crunchy potato rosti. **SERVES 4**

+ *Chipotle chilli in adobo sauce is available at most supermarkets
or at specialty stores.*

Crispy Potatoes

Shake up your regular side of fries with these equally crisp and golden sides. Serve them next to fish, schnitzel, or anything you would usually team with crunchy potatoes.

crunchy potato rosti

Preheat oven to 220°C (425°F). Place a 12 x ½-cup (125ml) capacity muffin tin in the oven to preheat. Grate **900g starchy roasting potatoes**, using a box grater. Place the grated potato between absorbent kitchen paper and squeeze out excess moisture. Combine the potato, **sea salt and cracked black pepper**. Remove the muffin tin from the oven and brush with ⅓ **cup (80ml) extra virgin olive oil**. Divide the potato between the tins and bake for 30 minutes or until crisp and golden. MAKES 12

salt and vinegar smashed potatoes

Cook **1kg baby new potatoes** in a large saucepan of simmering water for 20 minutes or until tender, then drain. Preheat oven to 240°C (464°F). Place potatoes on a baking tray lined with non-stick baking paper. Using a clean folded tea towel, crush each potato using your palm. Drizzle with **¼ cup (60ml) each of extra virgin olive oil and malt vinegar** and sprinkle with **sea salt and cracked black pepper**. Bake for 25 minutes or until crisp and golden. Drizzle with **extra malt vinegar**, if desired, to serve. SERVES 4

smoky potato fries

Preheat oven to 220°C (425°F). Place **800g starchy roasting potatoes that have been cut into fries** and **2 teaspoons each of table salt and smoked paprika** in a bowl and toss to coat. Add **2 tablespoons cornflour (cornstarch)** and toss to coat. Place the potatoes on a baking tray lined with non-stick baking paper and drizzle with **extra virgin olive oil**. Bake for 30–35 minutes or until crisp and golden. SERVES 4

herbed hash browns

Preheat oven to 220°C (425°F). Place **40g chopped unsalted butter, 2 tablespoons each of chopped dill leaves and chopped gherkins, 1 tablespoon chopped baby capers, sea salt and cracked black pepper** and **2 cups (500g) warm mashed potato** in a bowl and stir to combine. Place **1 cup (60g) panko breadcrumbs** in a separate bowl. Roll tablepsoonfuls of the potato mixture in the breadcrumbs to coat. Slightly flatten and place on a baking tray lined with non-stick baking paper. Drizzle with **extra virgin olive oil** and bake for 30 minutes or until crisp and golden. MAKES 24

Crispy

It's hard to resist the golden crumb of a schnitzel!
Get ready to meet your new family favourites – only crispier
and loaded with more personality than before thanks to new
ingredient heroes and fresh flavour twists. It's crunch time!

Schnitzels

chicken parma schnitzel

4 x 180g chicken breast fillets, trimmed and halved lengthways
16 basil leaves
8 slices buffalo mozzarella
cracked black pepper
8 slices prosciutto
3 cups (210g) fresh sourdough breadcrumbs
1 cup (80g) finely grated parmesan
⅓ cup (17g) finely chopped flat-leaf parsley leaves
extra virgin olive oil, for drizzling
basil leaves and basil and caper slaw (see *recipe*, page 68),
   to serve

TIP
Swap buffalo
mozzarella
for regular
mozzarella or
any other
soft cheese.

Preheat oven grill (broiler) to high.

Place the chicken on a baking tray lined with non-stick baking paper. Top each with 2 basil leaves and a slice of mozzarella, then sprinkle with pepper. Place 1 slice of prosciutto on top of each, folding them underneath the fillets to enclose.

Combine the breadcrumbs, parmesan and parsley in a bowl.

Top each chicken fillet with the breadcrumb mixture and press to coat. Drizzle generously with oil, then grill for 10–12 minutes or until golden and cooked through.

Serve with basil leaves and basil and caper slaw. **SERVES 4**

SCAN TO WATCH ME
CREATE THIS RECIPE

eggplant and pesto schnitzel

8 thick slices eggplant (aubergine), sliced lengthways
sea salt and cracked black pepper
extra virgin olive oil, for brushing
½ cup (135g) store-bought pesto
½ cup (110g) semi-dried tomatoes, chopped
1¼ cups (100g) finely grated parmesan
3 cups (210g) fresh sourdough breadcrumbs
1 egg, lightly beaten
basil and caper slaw (see *recipe*, page 68), to serve

TIP
To make fresh sourdough breadcrumbs, blitz fresh to 3-day-old sourdough in a food processor until coarsely chopped.

Preheat oven to 220°C (425°F).

Sprinkle the eggplant with salt and allow to drain for 5 minutes, then pat dry using absorbent kitchen paper.

Brush both sides of the eggplant slices with oil and place on a baking tray lined with non-stick baking paper. Bake for 15–20 minutes or until lightly golden. Remove from the oven.

Spread half of the eggplant slices with the pesto and top with the tomatoes. Sprinkle with 1 tablespoon parmesan, then top with the remaining eggplant slices to create eggplant 'sandwiches'.

Combine the breadcrumbs, the remaining parmesan and pepper.

Brush both sides of the eggplant sandwiches with the egg, then press firmly into the breadcrumb mixture to coat. **Return to the lined baking tray** and drizzle generously with oil. Bake for 15–20 minutes or until crisp and golden.

Serve with basil and caper slaw. **SERVES 4**

cauliflower blue cheese schnitzel

4 x 2cm-thick slices cauliflower (about 1 large cauliflower)
extra virgin olive oil, for brushing
sea salt and cracked black pepper
3 cups (210g) fresh sourdough breadcrumbs
100g blue cheese, crumbled
2 tablespoons finely chopped sage leaves, plus extra to serve
⅓ cup (40g) finely chopped walnuts
green apple and cucumber slaw (see _recipe_, page 69), to serve

TIP
If blue cheese isn't your thing, swap it for a milder cheese.

Preheat oven grill (broiler) to high.

Brush both sides of the cauliflower slices with oil and sprinkle with salt and pepper.

Place on a baking tray lined with non-stick baking paper and grill for 10–12 minutes or until tender and starting to brown. Remove from the oven.

Combine the breadcrumbs, blue cheese, sage, walnuts and pepper.

Press the breadcrumb mixture firmly on top of the cauliflower and drizzle generously with oil. Grill for 7–8 minutes or until crisp and golden.

Serve with the extra sage leaves and green apple and cucumber slaw. **SERVES 4**

caper and lemon fish schnitzel

4 x 175g skinless white fish fillets, trimmed
sea salt and cracked black pepper
3 cups (210g) fresh sourdough breadcrumbs
¼ cup (12g) chopped dill leaves
2 tablespoons baby capers, rinsed, drained and chopped
1 tablespoon finely grated lemon rind
2 eggs, lightly beaten
extra virgin olive oil, for drizzling
lemon wedges and minted celery slaw (see *recipe*, page 69),
    to serve

TIP
For the tastiest
results, choose
a firm-fleshed,
sustainable
fish fillet.

Preheat oven grill (broiler) to high.

Sprinkle both sides of the fish with salt and pepper. Combine the breadcrumbs, dill, capers and lemon rind.

Dip the fish into the egg, then press firmly in the breadcrumb mixture to coat.

Place on a baking tray lined with non-stick baking paper and drizzle generously with oil. Grill for 5–6 minutes each side or until crisp and golden.

Serve with lemon wedges and minted celery slaw. **SERVES 4**

crispy mushroom schnitzel

8 large field mushrooms, stems removed
extra virgin olive oil, for brushing
sea salt and cracked black pepper
3 cups (210g) fresh sourdough breadcrumbs
100g smoked cheddar+, grated
2 tablespoons chopped thyme leaves
2 eggs, lightly beaten
toasted sourdough slices and zucchini slaw (see *recipe*,
    page 68), to serve

TIP
Choose
larger field
mushrooms
to ensure they
retain their
'meaty' texture.

Preheat oven to 220°C (425°F).

Place the mushrooms, stem-side down, on a baking tray lined with non-stick baking paper. Brush with oil and sprinkle with salt and pepper. Top with non-stick baking paper and a second baking tray to help keep the mushrooms flat while they bake.

Bake for 40–45 minutes or until golden and the edges start to become crispy. Remove from the oven.

Combine the breadcrumbs, cheddar, thyme, salt and pepper.

Dip the mushrooms into the egg, then press firmly in the breadcrumb mixture to coat. Return to the lined baking tray and drizzle generously with oil. Bake for 15–20 minutes or until crisp and golden.

Serve with toasted sourdough slices and zucchini slaw. **SERVES 4**
+ *Find smoked cheddar at most supermarkets or at select grocers.*

Slaws

With their fresh hit of herbs, zingy burst of citrus or vinegar and crunchy cabbage, these reimagined slaws are a delicious way to balance a rich main.

basil and caper slaw

Combine **½ cup (125g) crème fraîche**, **1 tablespoon white wine vinegar** and **1 teaspoon finely grated lemon rind**. Place **300g shredded green cabbage, 2 tablespoons rinsed and drained baby capers** and **½ cup (10g) torn basil leaves** in a bowl. Pour the dressing over and toss to combine. SERVES 4

zucchini slaw

Whisk **⅓ cup (80ml) lemon juice, 2 tablespoons extra virgin olive oil, 2 teaspoons finely grated lemon rind, sea salt and cracked black pepper** together. Place **300g shredded green cabbage, 3 zucchinis (courgettes) that have been shredded using a julienne peeler** and **½ cup (24g) chopped dill leaves** in a bowl. Pour the dressing over and toss to combine. SERVES 4

green apple and cucumber slaw

Whisk **2 tablespoons each of honey, apple cider vinegar and seeded mustard** together. Place **300g shredded green cabbage, 2 cored and thinly sliced green apples, 2 Lebanese cucumbers that have been sliced lengthways on a mandoline** and **½ cup (12g) flat-leaf parsley leaves** in a bowl. Pour the dressing over and toss to combine. SERVES 4

minted celery slaw

Combine **½ cup (125ml) buttermilk, 2 teaspoons lemon juice, 1 teaspoon finely grated lemon rind, sea salt and cracked black pepper**. Place **300g shredded green cabbage, 4 trimmed celery stalks that have been shredded using a vegetable peeler** and **½ cup (8g) mint leaves** in a bowl. Pour the dressing over and toss to combine. SERVES 4

Skewers

Fire up the grill and get straight to the point with these sizzling skewers. With their charry, caramelised edges and 'why didn't I think of that?' combinations, they're a fast and super fun way to feed a crowd.

lemon, garlic and rosemary chicken skewers

800g chicken thigh fillets, trimmed and cut into pieces
sea salt and cracked black pepper
400g haloumi, cut into cubes
2 lemons, halved and thinly sliced into rounds
basil leaves, lemon wedges and olive and lemon brown rice salad
  (see *recipe*, page 82), to serve
lemon, garlic and rosemary marinade
⅓ cup (16g) rosemary leaves, roughly chopped
⅓ cup (80ml) extra virgin olive oil
4 cloves garlic, crushed
1 tablespoon lemon juice
2 teaspoons shredded lemon rind

TIP
To ensure everything cooks evenly, always use metal skewers.

To make the lemon, garlic and rosemary marinade, combine the rosemary, oil, garlic, lemon juice and lemon rind in a large bowl.

Add the chicken pieces, salt and pepper and mix to combine. Allow to marinate for 5 minutes.

Preheat oven grill (broiler) to high. Line a large baking tray with non-stick baking paper.

Thread the chicken, haloumi and lemon onto 8 metal skewers and place on the prepared tray. Grill for 13–15 minutes, or until golden and cooked through.

Serve with basil leaves, lemon wedges and olive and lemon brown rice salad. SERVES 4

SCAN TO WATCH ME
CREATE THIS RECIPE

ginger pork and pineapple skewers

600g pork fillet, trimmed and thinly sliced
250g pineapple, skin on and sliced into 8 thick wedges
sliced Lebanese cucumber, coriander (cilantro) and
   extra sliced long red chilli, to serve
ginger marinade
3 green onions (scallions), finely chopped
1 tablespoon finely grated ginger
2 cloves garlic, crushed
2 tablespoons fish sauce
⅓ cup (80g) firmly packed brown sugar
2 tablespoons extra virgin olive oil
chilli pickled carrot
2 tablespoons apple cider vinegar
2 teaspoons honey
1 long red chilli, sliced
4 carrots, peeled and shredded using a julienne peeler

To make the ginger marinade, combine the green onion, ginger, garlic, fish sauce, brown sugar and oil in a large bowl.

Add the pork and the pineapple and mix to combine. Refrigerate for 20 minutes to marinate.

To make the chilli pickled carrot, combine the vinegar, honey and chilli in a bowl. Add the carrot and toss to combine. Set aside.

Preheat oven grill (broiler) to high. Line a large baking tray with non-stick baking paper.

Thread the pork and pineapple onto 8 metal skewers and place on the prepared tray. Brush with any remaining ginger marinade and grill for 10–12 minutes or until just cooked through.

Serve with the chilli pickled carrot, cucumber, coriander and the extra chilli. **SERVES 4**

oregano fish and artichoke skewers with lemon olive dressing

750g skinless firm white fish fillets, trimmed and
  cut into 16 pieces
4 store-bought marinated artichoke hearts, halved
oregano oil
¼ cup (4g) oregano leaves
⅓ cup (80ml) extra virgin olive oil
1 teaspoon dried chilli flakes
sea salt and cracked black pepper
lemon olive dressing
¾ cup (120g) pitted green Sicilian olives, chopped
1 teaspoon shredded lemon rind
1 tablespoon lemon juice
⅓ cup (80ml) extra virgin olive oil

TIP
For the tastiest results, choose a firm-fleshed sustainable fish fillet.

To make the oregano oil, combine the oregano, oil, chilli, salt and pepper in a bowl. Set aside.

Preheat oven grill (broiler) to high. Line a large baking tray with non-stick baking paper.

Thread the fish and artichokes onto 8 metal skewers and place on the prepared tray. Brush generously with the oregano oil and grill for 5–6 minutes or until cooked through.

While the skewers are grilling, make the lemon olive dressing. Combine the olives, lemon rind, lemon juice and oil.

Spoon the lemon olive dressing over the skewers, to serve.

SERVES 4

sticky hoisin tempeh skewers

600g tempeh, cut into cubes
2 red onions, cut into thin wedges
grapeseed oil, for drizzling
coriander (cilantro), sliced long red chilli, roasted salted
    cashews and Asian rice and quinoa salad (see *recipe*, page 83),
    to serve
sticky hoisin marinade
½ cup (125ml) hoisin sauce
½ cup (180g) honey
¼ cup (60ml) soy sauce
2 tablespoons finely grated ginger
1½ tablespoons rice wine vinegar

TIP
Tempeh is a
protein-rich
plant-based
food made from
fermented
soybeans.
Swap it for firm
tofu, if you like.

To make the sticky hoisin marinade, combine the hoisin, honey,
soy sauce, ginger and vinegar in a bowl. Set aside.

Thread the tempeh and red onion onto 8 metal skewers. Spoon
the sticky hoisin marinade over and allow to marinate for
10 minutes.

Preheat oven grill (broiler) to high. Line a large baking tray with
non-stick baking paper.

Place the skewers on the prepared tray and drizzle with oil. Grill
for 16–18 minutes or until caramelised and the edges are charred.

Serve with coriander, chilli, cashews and the Asian rice and
quinoa salad. **SERVES 4**

pomegranate-glazed brussels sprout skewers with farro salad

⅓ cup (80g) firmly packed brown sugar
¼ cup (60ml) extra virgin olive oil
2 tablespoons pomegranate molasses
600g brussels sprouts (about 24), cut in half
sea salt and cracked black pepper
black sesame seeds and tahini dressing (see *recipe*, page 172),
  to serve
farro salad
3 cups (495g) cooked farro
1¼ cups (20g) mint leaves
½ cup (65g) roasted slivered almonds
⅓ cup (60g) pomegranate seeds

TIP
If you don't have farro, use freekeh instead. Find both at select supermarkets and specialty food stores.

Preheat oven grill (broiler) to high. Line a large baking tray with non-stick baking paper.

Combine the brown sugar, oil and pomegranate molasses in a bowl.

Thread the brussels sprout halves onto 8 metal skewers and place on the prepared tray. Spoon the pomegranate glaze over and sprinkle with salt and pepper. Grill for 13–15 minutes or until caramelised and the edges are charred.

While the brussels sprouts are grilling, make the farro salad. Combine the farro, mint, almonds and pomegranate.

Sprinkle the brussels sprout skewers with sesame seeds. Serve with the farro salad and tahini dressing. **SERVES 4**

Grain Salads

With a flutter of fresh herbs, toasted nuts and some pantry power, you can whip up these texturally-charged, nice-for-you bowls – the tastiest base for any meal!

olive and lemon brown rice salad

Heat a small saucepan over low heat. Add **1 cup (60g) pitted and sliced green Sicilian olives**, **2 tablespoons shredded lemon rind** and **¼ cup (60ml) extra virgin olive oil** and cook for 3–4 minutes. Add **2 tablespoons lemon juice** and stir to combine. Mix **3 cups (495g) cooked brown rice, 1 cup (20g) basil leaves** and the lemon olive dressing and toss to combine.

SERVES 4 AS A SIDE

Asian rice and quinoa salad

Combine **2 tablespoons each of grapeseed oil and mirin (Japanese rice wine)** and **1 tablespoon soy sauce**. Add **2 chopped green onions (scallions)** and **1 long deseeded and chopped red chilli** and toss to combine. Mix **1½ cups (245g) cooked jasmine rice**, **1½ cups (210g) cooked quinoa**, **1 cup (16g) coriander (cilantro) leaves** and the chilli soy dressing and toss to combine. Sprinkle with **½ cup (50g) roasted and chopped salted cashews**. SERVES 4 AS A SIDE

freekeh salad

Combine **2 tablespoons each of lemon juice and extra virgin olive oil**, **2 teaspoons wholegrain mustard** and **1 teaspoon honey**. Mix **3 cups (480g) cooked freekeh**, **1 cup (52g) chopped flat-leaf parsley leaves** and the honey mustard dressing and toss to combine. Sprinkle with **⅓ cup (45g) chopped pistachios**. SERVES 4 AS A SIDE

red quinoa and mint salad

Combine **2 tablespoons red wine vinegar** and **1 tablespoon Dijon mustard** together. Add **⅓ cup (45g) dried cranberries** and allow to stand for 5 minutes or until softened. Mix **3 cups (420g) cooked red quinoa**, **1 cup (16g) mint leaves** and the dressing and toss to combine. Sprinkle with **⅓ cup (50g) chopped roasted almonds**. SERVES 4 AS A SIDE

Meatballs

No longer confined to nonna's spaghetti, these comforting meatballs have travelled the globe and returned as saucy flavour bombs that can stand on their own or take that bowl of noodles, rice or pasta to delicious new heights.

Thai red curry meatballs

600g beef mince
2 tablespoons Thai red curry paste
1½ cups (250g) cooked jasmine rice
1 tablespoon finely grated ginger
¼ cup (13g) chopped coriander (cilantro) leaves
1 egg
1 tablespoon grapeseed oil
thinly sliced green onion (scallion), sliced long red chilli,
    extra coriander (cilantro) and sesame ginger noodles
    (see *recipe*, page 98), to serve
Thai red curry sauce
2 tablespoons Thai red curry paste, extra
1½ cups (375ml) coconut cream
2 tablespoons lime juice
1 tablespoon fish sauce

TIP
For the tastiest
meatballs,
choose a
good-quality
red curry paste.

Place the mince, curry paste, rice, ginger, coriander and egg in
a bowl and mix to combine. Shape the mixture into 16 x ¼-cup
meatballs and set aside.

To make the Thai red curry sauce, combine the extra curry paste
and coconut cream. Set aside.

Heat a large deep frying pan over medium-high heat.

Add the oil and meatballs and cook for 3 minutes each side or
until browned all over.

Add the Thai red curry sauce and bring to a simmer. Cook for
7–8 minutes, turning the meatballs halfway, until the sauce has
reduced and the meatballs are cooked through. Add the lime juice
and fish sauce and gently stir to combine.

Divide between bowls and top with the green onion, chilli and
extra coriander. Serve with sesame ginger noodles. **SERVES 4**

kale, lemon and parmesan meatballs

8 cups (280g) firmly packed finely shredded kale leaves

1 x 400g can white (cannellini) beans, rinsed, drained
and roughly mashed

1 tablespoon finely grated lemon rind

1½ cups (360g) fresh ricotta

1 egg

1½ cups (180g) almond meal (ground almonds)

½ cup (40g) finely grated parmesan, plus extra to serve

sea salt and cracked black pepper

sage and garlic sauce

1 tablespoon extra virgin olive oil

12 sage leaves

4 cloves garlic, sliced

2 cups (500g) diced canned tomatoes

½ cup (125ml) good-quality vegetable or chicken stock

TIP
I love to serve these meatballs with pasta or crusty bread for mopping up all that delicious sauce!

Place the kale in a bowl and cover with boiling water. Allow to stand for 3 minutes, then drain well. Place between absorbent kitchen paper and press to drain any excess moisture.

Combine the kale, beans, rind, ricotta, egg, almond meal, parmesan, salt and pepper. Shape the mixture into 16 x ¼-cup meatballs.

Preheat oven to 220°C (440°F).

To make the sage and garlic sauce, heat a large ovenproof frying pan over medium-high heat. Add the oil, sage and garlic and cook for 30 seconds or until soft. Add the tomatoes and stock, bring to a simmer and cook for 5 minutes. Add the meatballs and transfer the pan to the oven. Bake for 20–25 minutes or until cooked through.

Serve with extra parmesan. **SERVES 4**

SCAN TO WATCH ME
CREATE THIS RECIPE

baked chicken, leek and tarragon meatballs

700g chicken mince
1 cup (120g) almond meal (ground almonds)
1 tablespoon finely grated lemon rind
1 egg
2 tablespoons chopped tarragon leaves
sea salt and cracked black pepper
peppered spaghetti (see *recipe*, page 99), to serve
leek and tarragon sauce
2 tablespoons extra virgin olive oil
2 leeks, trimmed and thinly sliced
½ cup (125ml) dry white wine (optional)
1 cup (250ml) good-quality chicken stock
1 tablespoon Dijon mustard
1 cup (250ml) pure cream
4 sprigs tarragon

TIP
You could also serve these tasty gluten-free meatballs with your favourite gluten-free pasta.

Preheat oven to 200°C (400°F).

Place the mince, almond meal, lemon rind, egg, tarragon, salt and pepper in a bowl and mix to combine. Roll 2 heaped tablespoons of the mixture into balls and set aside.

To make the leek and tarragon sauce, heat a large ovenproof frying pan over medium heat.

Add the oil and leeks and cook for 6 minutes or until golden. Pour in the wine and cook for 1 minute. Add the stock, mustard, cream and tarragon. Increase the heat to a simmer and cook for 5–8 minutes. Add the meatballs and gently stir to coat.

Transfer the pan to the oven and bake for 15 minutes or until golden and cooked through.

Divide between bowls and serve with peppered spaghetti. **SERVES 4**

feta-stuffed lamb meatballs

600g lamb mince
1½ cups (210g) cooked quinoa
1 egg
2 teaspoons finely grated lemon rind
⅓ cup (16g) chopped dill leaves
⅓ cup (18g) chopped mint leaves
sea salt and cracked black pepper
120g firm feta, cut into 8 cubes
2 tablespoons extra virgin olive oil
2 x 400g cans cherry tomatoes
½ cup (125ml) good-quality beef stock
6 sprigs oregano, plus extra to serve
olive pasta (see *recipe*, page 99), to serve

TIP
These meatballs are great to make ahead – simply roll and place on a lined tray in the refrigerator the day before.

Place the mince, quinoa, egg, lemon rind, dill, mint, salt and pepper in a bowl and mix to combine.

Shape 8 x ½-cupfuls of the mixture into flat patties. Place a piece of feta in the centre of each and fold the edges over to enclose. Roll into rounds.

Heat a large frying pan over medium-high heat.

Add the oil and cook the meatballs for 6–8 minutes or until well browned, turning frequently.

Add the tomatoes, stock and oregano and reduce the heat to a simmer. Cook for 10–12 minutes or until the sauce has thickened slightly and the meatballs are cooked through.

Divide between bowls and top with the extra oregano. Serve with the olive pasta. SERVES 4

spicy cashew tofu meatballs

600g firm tofu, drained and grated

1 small onion, finely grated

1 cup (120g) grated carrot

1 teaspoon dried chilli flakes

⅓ cup (80g) cashew butter

⅓ cup (35g) ground linseeds (linseed meal)

2 tablespoons white chia seeds

sea salt and cracked black pepper

grapeseed oil, for brushing

½ cup (70g) chopped roasted unsalted cashews

thinly sliced green onion (scallion), thinly sliced long red chilli
   and coriander (cilantro), to serve

soy glaze

¾ cup (180ml) mirin (Japanese rice wine)

¼ cup (60ml) soy sauce

¼ cup (60ml) pure maple syrup

1 tablespoon Asian chilli sauce

1 tablespoon coarsely grated ginger

TIP
Use wet hands
to help you roll
these meatballs.

Place the grated tofu between sheets of absorbent kitchen paper
and press to drain any excess moisture.

Combine the tofu, onion, carrot, chilli flakes, cashew butter,
linseeds, chia seeds, salt and pepper. Set aside for 5 minutes or
until the mixture is firm.

Preheat oven to 220°C (440°F).

Press heaped tablespoons of the mixture into balls. Place on a
baking tray lined with non-stick baking paper. Brush with oil and
bake for 25–30 minutes, turning halfway, or until golden.

To make the soy glaze, combine the mirin, soy sauce, maple syrup,
chilli sauce and ginger in a frying pan over medium-high heat. Cook
for 4–5 minutes or until slightly thickened. Add the tofu meatballs
and cashews and toss to coat.

Serve with green onion, chilli and coriander. **SERVES 4**

Pasta + Noodles

These deliciously diverse strands make the perfect pairing for meatballs or a tasty tangle for your favourite saucy accompaniment.

sesame ginger noodles

Place **300g dried rice noodles** in a bowl and cover with **boiling water**. Allow to stand for 8 minutes or until just soft, then drain. Place **2 tablespoons grapeseed oil** and **1 tablespoon sesame oil** in a small frying pan over medium-low heat. Add **2 tablespoons coarsely grated ginger** and cook for 5 minutes or until lightly browned. Add **1 tablespoon sesame seeds** and cook for 1 minute. Spoon the sesame ginger oil over the noodles and top with **sliced green onion (scallion)**. SERVES 4

peppered spaghetti

Cook **300g dried spaghetti** in a saucepan of boiling salted water until al dente. Drain, **reserving ¼ cup (60ml) of pasta water** and set aside. Return saucepan to medium-high heat. Add the **reserved pasta water, 80g unsalted butter** and **2 teaspoons cracked black pepper** and cook for 1 minute or until fragrant. Return pasta to the pan with **1½ cups (120g) finely grated parmesan** and toss to coat. SERVES 4

olive pasta

Cook **300g dried rigatoni** in a saucepan of boiling salted water until al dente. Drain and set aside. Return saucepan to medium-high heat. Add **2 tablespoons each of extra virgin olive oil and oregano leaves, ⅓ cup (40g) sliced pitted kalamata olives** and **3 cloves sliced garlic.** Cook for 1–2 minutes or until the garlic is golden. Return pasta to the pan and add **¼ cup (5g) chopped basil leaves, sea salt and cracked black pepper**. Toss to coat. Serve with **lemon wedges**. SERVES 4

zucchini noodles with chilli garlic oil

Slice **3 zucchinis (courgettes)** into thin strips, using a julienne peeler. Heat **2 tablespoons extra virgin olive oil** in a saucepan over medium heat. Add **3 cloves sliced garlic** and **2 deseeded and chopped red chillies**. Cook for 2 minutes or until fragrant. Pour the chilli garlic oil over the zucchini noodles and sprinkle with **sea salt and cracked black pepper**. SERVES 4

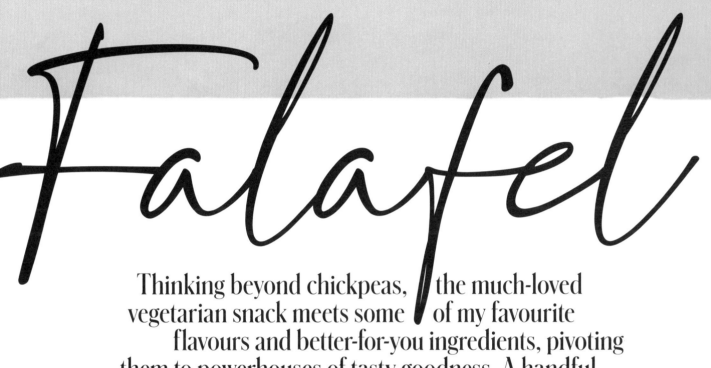

Falafel

Thinking beyond chickpeas, the much-loved vegetarian snack meets some of my favourite flavours and better-for-you ingredients, pivoting them to powerhouses of tasty goodness. A handful of shortcuts and punchy dips seal the deal.

smoky chipotle black bean falafel

2 x 400g cans chickpeas (garbanzo beans), rinsed and drained
1 x 400g can black beans, rinsed and drained
1 cup (24g) flat-leaf parsley leaves
1 cup (16g) coriander (cilantro) leaves
1½ red onions, finely chopped
2 cloves garlic, finely chopped
2 teaspoons smoked paprika
2 tablespoons extra virgin olive oil, plus extra for brushing
2 tablespoons chopped chipotle chillies in adobo sauce+
2 tablespoons plain (all-purpose) flour
½ teaspoon baking powder
sea salt and cracked black pepper
warmed pita bread, sliced avocado, sliced tomato, extra coriander (cilantro), smoky spiced hummus (see *recipe*, page 113) and lime wedges, to serve

Preheat oven to 220°C (425°F).

Place the chickpeas and black beans on a baking tray lined with non-stick baking paper. Bake for 20 minutes or until slightly dried.

Transfer the chickpeas and black beans to a food processor. Add the parsley, coriander, onion, garlic, paprika, oil, chipotle chillies, flour, baking powder, salt and pepper and process until very finely chopped.

Roll 2 tablespoonfuls of the mixture into patties and place on a baking tray lined with non-stick baking paper. Brush the patties with oil and bake for 25 minutes or until golden and crisp.

Serve the falafel with pita bread, avocado, tomato, the extra coriander, smoky spiced hummus and lime wedges. **MAKES 16**

+ *Chipotle chilli in adobo sauce is available at most supermarkets or at specialty stores.*

pea and quinoa falafel

3 cups (420g) frozen peas, thawed
3 cups (420g) cooked quinoa
1½ cups (24g) mint leaves
1 cup (24g) flat-leaf parsley leaves
1 onion, finely chopped
2 cloves garlic, finely chopped
sea salt and cracked black pepper
extra virgin olive oil, for brushing
thinly sliced watermelon radish, wild leaf rocket (arugula) and
    marinated feta, to serve

TIP
With help from some standby frozen quinoa and peas, you can whip these up in no time!

Preheat oven to 220°C (425°F).

Place the peas between absorbent kitchen paper and press to drain any excess moisture.

Place the peas, quinoa, mint, parsley, onion, garlic, salt and pepper in a food processor and process until very finely chopped.

Roll 2 tablespoonfuls of the mixture into patties and place on a baking tray lined with non-stick baking paper. Brush each patty with oil and bake for 35–40 minutes or until golden and crisp.

Divide the falafel between plates and serve with watermelon radish, rocket and marinated feta. **MAKES 16**

quick falafel

4 x 400g cans chickpeas (garbanzo beans), rinsed and drained
1 onion, finely chopped
1 cup (24g) flat-leaf parsley leaves
1 cup (16g) coriander (cilantro) leaves
2 tablespoons extra virgin olive oil, plus extra for brushing
2 tablespoons plain (all-purpose) flour
2 teaspoons ground cumin
3 cloves garlic, finely chopped
½ teaspoon baking powder
sea salt and cracked black pepper
pita bread, minted tahini (see *recipe*, page 112), sliced baby
  cucumbers, sliced tomatoes, red-veined sorrel, sumac[+]
  and lemon wedges, to serve

TIP
Serve these
with any
store-bought
dips that catch
your eye.

Preheat oven to 220°C (425°F).
   Place the chickpeas on a baking tray and bake for 20 minutes
or until slightly dried.
   Transfer the chickpeas to a food processor. Add the onion,
parsley, coriander, oil, flour, cumin, garlic, baking powder, salt and
pepper and process until very finely chopped.
   Shape 2 tablespoonfuls of the mixture into patties and place on
a baking tray lined with non-stick baking paper. Brush each patty
with oil and bake for 25 minutes or until golden and crisp.
   Place the pita breads on serving plates and top with minted
tahini, baby cucumbers, tomato, the falafel and red-veined sorrel.
Sprinkle with sumac and serve with lemon wedges. **MAKES 16**
+ *Tangy, lemony sumac is found in the spice section of most
supermarkets, or in select grocers and specialty stores.*

edamame falafel

2 x 400g cans chickpeas (garbanzo beans), rinsed and drained
3 cups (420g) frozen shelled edamame beans, thawed
1 cup (24g) flat-leaf parsley leaves
2½ tablespoons chopped store-bought pickled ginger
2 tablespoons white miso paste
2 tablespoons grapeseed oil, plus extra for brushing
cracked black pepper
½ teaspoon baking powder
300g firm tofu, drained and finely crumbled
thinly sliced Lebanese cucumber, salad leaves, black sesame
    seeds, extra store-bought pickled ginger, shiso leaves and
    coriander yoghurt (see *recipe*, page 113), to serve

TIP
We use white
(shiro) miso
paste for its more
delicate flavour.
Find it at select
supermarkets or
Asian grocers.

Preheat oven to 220°C (425°F).

Place the chickpeas on a baking tray and bake for 20 minutes
or until slightly dried.

Transfer the chickpeas to a food processor. Add the edamame,
parsley, pickled ginger, miso, oil, pepper and baking powder and
process until very finely chopped. Add the tofu and mix to combine.

Shape 2 tablespoonfuls of the mixture into patties and place on a
baking tray lined with non-stick baking paper. Brush each patty with
oil and bake for 25–30 minutes or until golden and crisp.

Divide the falafel between plates and serve with cucumber,
salad leaves, black sesame seeds, extra pickled ginger, shiso and
coriander yoghurt. **MAKES 20**

spiced sweet potato falafel

2 x 400g cans chickpeas (garbanzo beans), rinsed and drained
3 cups (410g) firmly packed grated orange sweet potato (kumara)
1½ cups (24g) coriander (cilantro) leaves
1½ cups (24g) mint leaves
3 green onions (scallions), sliced
1½ tablespoons harissa paste+
2 tablespoons plain (all-purpose) flour
½ teaspoon baking powder
sea salt and cracked black pepper
extra virgin olive oil, for brushing
butter lettuce leaves, tomato and mint salsa (see *recipe*,
   page 112), coriander yoghurt (see *recipe*, page 113) and
   coriander (cilantro), to serve

TIP
These falafel make a great party snack when passed around a crowd.

Preheat oven to 220°C (440°F).

Place the chickpeas on a baking tray and bake for 20 minutes or until slightly dried.

Transfer the chickpeas to a food processor. Add the sweet potato, coriander, mint, green onion, harissa, flour, baking powder, salt and pepper and process until very finely chopped.

Shape 2 tablespoonfuls of the mixture into patties and place on a baking tray lined with non-stick baking paper. Brush each patty with oil and bake for 30 minutes or until golden and crisp.

Place the butter lettuce leaves on serving plates and top with tomato and mint salsa, the falafel, coriander yoghurt and coriander.

MAKES 16

+ Harissa, a northern African chilli paste, can be found at select supermarkets and specialty stores.

Dips

Brighten up your falafel with a rainbow of fast, fresher-than-fresh, Middle Eastern-inspired sides. Just the burst of flavour your table needed!

minted tahini

Place ⅔ **cup (180g) hulled tahini**, ⅓ **cup (80ml) each of lemon juice and water**, ½ **cup (8g) mint leaves, sea salt and cracked black pepper** into a blender and blend until smooth. MAKES 1½ CUPS

tomato and mint salsa

Place **2 ripe diced tomatoes, 1 tablespoon each of extra virgin olive oil, lemon juice and mint leaves, sea salt and cracked black pepper** in a bowl and mix to combine. Sprinkle with **finely grated lemon rind**. MAKES 1½ CUPS

coriander yoghurt

Place **1 cup (250g) plain thick yoghurt**, **½ cup (26g) finely chopped coriander (cilantro) leaves**, **1 teaspoon finely grated lemon rind**, **sea salt and cracked black pepper** in a bowl and mix to combine. **MAKES 1½ CUPS**

smoky spiced hummus

Place **2 x 400g cans rinsed and drained chickpeas (garbanzo beans)**, **¼ cup (70g) hulled tahini**, **2 cloves crushed garlic**, **⅓ cup (80ml) lemon juice**, **¼ cup (60ml) extra virgin olive oil**, **sea salt and cracked black pepper** in a food processor and process until smooth. Add **⅓ cup (80ml) water** and process to combine. Refrigerate for 1 hour or until chilled. Combine **2 tablespoons extra virgin olive oil**, **2 teaspoons harissa paste** and **1 teaspoon smoked paprika**. Spoon the harissa oil over the hummus, before serving. **MAKES 2½ CUPS**

Coconut

Creamy curries sing with roasty, toasty spices and star some new heavy-lifting ingredients and textural twists. The result is comforting bowls featuring pools of fragrant flavour for rice and noodles to soak up.

Curries

chicken and pumpkin korma

2 tablespoons grapeseed oil

2 onions, cut into thin wedges

2 teaspoons garam masala

2 teaspoons ground cumin

1 teaspoon ground turmeric

2 tablespoons desiccated coconut

1 tablespoon finely grated ginger

4 vine-ripened tomatoes, chopped

2 long green chillies, sliced

800g pumpkin, peeled, deseeded and cut into small chunks

1 cup (250ml) good-quality chicken stock

4 x 180g chicken breast fillets, trimmed and cut into thirds

plain thick yoghurt, chopped roasted salted cashews,
   coriander (cilantro), extra sliced long green chilli and
   spiced pistachio rice (see *recipe*, page 129), to serve

TIP
Use sweet
potato instead
of pumpkin if
you have some
at home already.

Heat a large deep frying pan over medium heat.

Add the oil, onion, garam masala, cumin and turmeric and cook for 2 minutes or until fragrant. Add the coconut and ginger and cook, stirring constantly, for 1 minute. Add the tomatoes and chilli and cook for 5 minutes. Add the pumpkin and stock and stir to combine. Cover with a tight-fitting lid, bring to a simmer and cook for 10 minutes or until the pumpkin starts to soften. Remove the lid.

Add the chicken and cook for 8–10 minutes or until cooked through, turning halfway.

Divide the curry between bowls and serve with yoghurt, cashews, coriander, the extra chilli and spiced pistachio rice. **SERVES 4**

stir-fried green curry of greens

2 tablespoons grapeseed oil
2 onions, cut into thin wedges
½ cup (150g) Thai green curry paste
500g firm tofu, drained and cut into cubes
2 tablespoons shredded ginger
420g broccolini (sprouting broccoli), trimmed and halved
300g sugar snap peas, trimmed
450g gai lan (Chinese broccoli), trimmed and halved
½ cup (125ml) coconut cream
coriander (cilantro), sliced long green chilli and coconut chilli
   rice (see *recipe*, page 128), to serve

TIP
Keep the
vegies crunchy
and green for
maximum
flavour and
texture.

Heat a wok or large deep frying pan over high heat.

Add 1 tablespoon of the oil, the onions and the curry paste. Cook for 2 minutes or until the onions start to colour and turn fragrant. Add the tofu and cook for 2 minutes. Remove from the pan.

Add the remaining 1 tablespoon of oil to the pan. Add the ginger and cook for 30 seconds. Add the broccolini, sugar snap peas and gai lan and cook for 3–4 minutes or until they start to colour. Return the tofu and onions to the pan.

Pour in the coconut cream and gently stir to coat. Cook for 2 minutes or until warm.

Serve with coriander, green chilli and coconut chilli rice. **SERVES 4**

Thai coconut red curry salmon

⅓ cup (100g) Thai red curry paste
6 Thai lime leaves, lightly crushed
1 tablespoon finely grated ginger
1 tablespoon grapeseed oil
2 cups (500ml) coconut milk
600g skinless salmon fillet, cut into 8 pieces
250g snow peas (mange tout), trimmed and halved lengthways
1 tablespoon fish sauce
1 tablespoon lime juice
thinly sliced Thai lime leaves, Thai basil leaves, lime wedges and
    cashew and coriander brown rice (see *recipe*, page 128),
    to serve

TIP
The squeeze of lime adds an addictive tang to the creamy curry, helping to balance the richness.

Heat a wok or large deep frying pan over medium heat.
  Add the curry paste, lime leaves, ginger and oil and cook for 1–2 minutes or until fragrant.
  Pour in the coconut milk, bring to a simmer and cook for 5 minutes, stirring occasionally.
  Add the salmon and cook for 2 minutes. Turn the salmon over and add the snow peas. Cook for a further 2 minutes or until the salmon is cooked to your liking. Add the fish sauce and lime juice and gently stir to combine.
  Serve with lime leaves, Thai basil, lime wedges and cashew and coriander brown rice. **SERVES 4**

spicy peanut cauliflower curry

¾ cup (210g) crunchy natural peanut butter
¾ cup (180ml) coconut cream
2 tablespoons finely grated ginger
2 tablespoons kecap manis (sweet soy sauce), plus extra
for drizzling
½ teaspoon ground turmeric
sea salt and cracked black pepper
1kg cauliflower florets
1 x 400g can chickpeas (garbanzo beans), rinsed and drained
2 onions, cut into thin wedges
2 long red chillies, sliced
coriander (cilantro) and spiced basmati rice (see *recipe*,
page 129), to serve

TIP
To keep this
family-friendly,
go easy on the
chilli or leave it
out altogether.

Preheat oven to 200°C (400°F). Line 2 large baking trays with
non-stick baking paper.

Combine the peanut butter, coconut cream, ginger, kecap manis,
turmeric, salt and pepper in a large bowl. Add the cauliflower,
chickpeas and onions and gently toss to combine.

Place the peanut cauliflower mixture onto the prepared trays
and bake for 25 minutes.

Add the chilli and bake for a further 20 minutes or until golden,
turning halfway.

Divide between bowls, drizzle with the extra kecap manis and
serve with coriander and spiced basmati rice. **SERVES 4**

SCAN TO WATCH ME
CREATE THIS RECIPE

cashew and ginger curry noodles

200g dried rice noodles or egg noodles
1 tablespoon grapeseed oil
2 tablespoons finely grated ginger
2 cloves garlic, chopped
⅓ cup (100g) Thai red curry paste
1 cup (250ml) water
2 cups (500ml) coconut milk
200g green beans, trimmed and halved lengthways
1 tablespoon fish sauce or coconut aminos[+]
sliced hard-boiled egg, thinly sliced long red chilli, thinly sliced
   green onion (scallion), bean sprouts and roasted salted
   cashews, to serve

TIP
For a vegan
version, leave
out the egg
and use
rice noodles.

Cook the noodles according to the packet instructions. Refresh
under cold water, drain and set aside.
   Heat a wok or large deep frying pan over medium-high heat.
   Add the oil, ginger, garlic and curry paste and cook for 2 minutes
or until fragrant. Pour in the water and coconut milk and bring to
a simmer. Add the beans and cook for 2–3 minutes. Add the fish
sauce and noodles and toss to coat.
   Divide the noodles between bowls and top with hard-boiled egg,
chilli, green onion and bean sprouts. Serve with cashews. **SERVES 4**
+ *Made from the sap of coconut flowers, coconut aminos is a vegan,
soy-free alternative to soy sauce and fish sauce. Find it in the Asian
section of select supermarkets or at Asian grocers.*

Rices

Laced with toasted nuts and seeds, warm spices and pops of fruit, these rice dishes make an exciting pairing for curries and stir-fries, but can also hold their own as a light meal.

cashew and coriander brown rice

Heat a large non-stick frying pan over medium heat. Add **2 tablespoons grapeseed oil, ½ cup (75g) roasted salted cashews** and **1 tablespoon sesame seeds** and cook for 1 minute or until golden. Add **3½ cups (580g) cooked brown rice** and **sea salt flakes** and stir to combine. Cook for 2 minutes or until warm. Serve with **½ cup (26g) chopped coriander (cilantro) leaves**. SERVES 4

coconut chilli rice

Heat a large non-stick frying pan over medium heat. Add **¾ cup (180ml) coconut milk** and **1 sliced long green chilli** and cook for 3–4 minutes. Add **3½ cups (575g) cooked jasmine rice** and **sea salt flakes** and stir to combine. Cook for 2 minutes or until warm. SERVES 4

spiced basmati rice

Heat a large non-stick frying pan over medium heat. Add **2 tablespoons grapeseed oil**, **3 bruised cardamom pods, ½ cup (80g) blanched almonds, a pinch of saffron threads** and **sea salt flakes** and cook for 2 minutes. Add **3 cups (495g) cooked basmati rice** and **1 x 400g can rinsed and drained lentils** and stir to combine. Cook for 2 minutes or until warm. Remove from the heat, add **¼ cup (35g) currants** and **2 tablespoons chopped flat-leaf parsley leaves** and gently toss to combine. SERVES 4

spiced pistachio rice

Heat a large non-stick frying pan over medium heat. Add **2 tablespoons grapeseed oil**, **2 teaspoons garam masala** and **⅓ cup (50g) salted pistachios** and cook for 1 minute. Add **4 cups (520g) cooked brown basmati rice** and stir to combine. Cook for 2 minutes or until warm. Remove from the heat, drizzle with **1 tablespoon pomegranate molasses** and stir to combine. SERVES 4

Noodles

What could be more comforting than curling up with a bowl of noodles that glisten under an umami-rich sauce, all tangled up with crunchy greens? Whether you like yours hot or cold, these speedy strands will satisfy everyone.

noodle salad with chilli tofu

200g dried rice vermicelli
3 carrots, thinly shredded using a julienne peeler
160g bean sprouts
1 cup (16g) coriander (cilantro) leaves
1 cup (16g) mint leaves
½ red onion, thinly sliced
2 long red chillies, thinly sliced
½ cup (70g) roasted salted peanuts
chilli tofu
600g firm tofu, drained and cut into cubes
½ cup (150g) Asian chilli jam+
1 tablespoon grapeseed oil
3 green onions (scallions), chopped
ginger soy dressing
⅓ cup (80ml) lime juice
2 tablespoons soy sauce
1 tablespoon finely grated ginger

TIP
These noodles are just as tasty for lunch the next day – in fact – the flavours deepen overnight.

Cook the noodles according to the packet instructions. Refresh under cold water, drain and set aside.

To make the chilli tofu, preheat oven grill (broiler) to medium-high.

Place the tofu, chilli jam and oil in a bowl and gently toss to coat. Place the tofu on a baking tray lined with non-stick baking paper and grill for 6–7 minutes. Add the green onion and grill for a further 6–7 minutes or until the tofu is crisp and golden.

While the tofu is grilling, make the ginger soy dressing. Combine the lime juice, soy sauce and ginger.

Divide the noodles, carrot, bean sprouts, coriander, mint and onion between bowls. Pour the ginger soy dressing over and toss to combine. Top with the chilli tofu, chilli and peanuts. **SERVES 4**
+ *Find Asian chilli jam in the Asian section of select supermarkets or at Asian grocers. Where possible, choose a good-quality one.*

chicken and edamame soba salad

400g dried soba noodles
2 cups (280g) frozen shelled edamame beans, thawed
3 green onions (scallions), thinly sliced
4 cups (100g) baby spinach leaves
3 x cooked chicken breast fillets, thinly sliced
⅓ cup (30g) store-bought pickled ginger
2 tablespoons toasted sesame seeds
miso dressing
⅓ cup (80ml) mirin (Japanese rice wine)
¼ cup (55g) white miso paste
2 tablespoons rice wine vinegar
1 tablespoon sesame oil

TIP
I like to switch this recipe up by replacing the chicken with grilled salmon or tofu from time to time.

To make the miso dressing, whisk the mirin, miso, rice wine vinegar and sesame oil together to combine. Set aside.

Cook the noodles according to the packet instructions. Refresh under cold water, then drain.

Divide the noodles, edamame, green onion, baby spinach and chicken between bowls. Pour the miso dressing over and toss to combine. Top with the pickled ginger and toasted sesame seeds.

SERVES 4

crispy kimchi noodle pancake

200g dried rice noodles
1 cup (280g) chopped kimchi, plus extra to serve
2 tablespoons rice flour
1 tablespoon toasted sesame seeds
1 tablespoon finely grated ginger
2 tablespoons grapeseed oil
shiso leaves, to serve (optional)
pickled cucumber salad
½ cup (125ml) rice wine vinegar
1 tablespoon caster (superfine) sugar
2 Lebanese cucumbers, thinly sliced
4 green onions (scallions), thinly sliced

TIP
Be sure to cook the pancake for the full 8 minutes to let it really crisp up.

To make the pickled cucumber salad, mix the rice wine vinegar and sugar together.

Combine the cucumber and green onion in a bowl and pour the dressing over. Toss to combine and set aside.

Cook the noodles according to the packet instructions. Refresh under cold water, then drain. Spread the noodles out onto a baking tray lined with non-stick paper. Allow to cool for 5 minutes.

Add the kimchi, rice flour, sesame seeds and ginger to the cooled noodles. Toss to combine.

Heat a large non-stick frying pan over medium heat.

Add the oil and the noodle mixture, spreading it out into a pancake shape with a spatula. Cook the noodle pancake for 8 minutes each side or until crisp and golden.

Slice into wedges and serve with the pickled cucumber salad, the extra kimchi and shiso leaves, if desired. **SERVES 4**

saucy egg noodles

400g fresh egg noodles

2 cloves garlic, crushed

4 green onions (scallions), sliced

500g pork or chicken mince

2 cups (500ml) good-quality chicken stock

extra sliced green onion (scallion), sliced long red chilli and
  chopped roasted salted peanuts, to serve

spicy peanut sauce

¼ cup (70g) smooth natural peanut butter or hulled tahini

¼ cup (60ml) hoisin sauce

¼ cup (60ml) soy sauce

2 teaspoons sesame oil

1 tablespoon store-bought chilli oil

1 tablespoon honey

TIP
To prevent the
noodles from
sticking together,
drain them and
stir in a little oil,
then spread
them out on a
baking tray.

Cook the noodles according to the packet instructions. Refresh
under cold water, drain and set aside.

To make the spicy peanut sauce, place the peanut butter,
hoisin, soy sauce, sesame oil, chilli oil and honey in a bowl and
whisk to combine.

Heat a large frying pan over medium-high heat.

Add half the spicy peanut sauce, the garlic and green onion
and cook for 1 minute. Add the mince and cook for 7–8 minutes
or until well browned.

Place the stock in a small saucepan over medium-low heat.
Cook for 5 minutes or until hot. Add the remaining spicy peanut
sauce and stir until heated through and combined.

To serve, divide the spicy peanut sauce between bowls and
add the hot noodles. Top with the mince, extra green onion,
red chilli and roasted peanuts. **SERVES 4**

SCAN TO WATCH ME
CREATE THIS RECIPE

fiery Sichuan peanut chilli noodles

400g fresh egg noodles
¼ cup (60ml) soy sauce
2 tablespoons smooth natural peanut butter
1 teaspoon caster (superfine) sugar
4 green onions (scallions), white and green parts separated
  and shredded
4 cloves garlic, finely chopped
600g gai lan (Chinese broccoli), trimmed and chopped
⅓ cup (80ml) Chinese cooking wine
⅓ cup (80g) roughly chopped roasted salted peanuts
fiery Sichuan oil
⅓ cup (80ml) grapeseed oil
1 tablespoon Sichuan peppercorns, crushed
1 tablespoon dried chilli flakes

To make the fiery Sichuan oil, place the oil, peppercorns and chilli
in a small saucepan over medium-low heat and cook for 2 minutes.
Remove from the heat and allow to infuse for 2 minutes.

Cook the noodles according to the packet instructions. Refresh
under cold water, drain and set aside.

Whisk the soy sauce, peanut butter and sugar together. Set aside.

Heat a large deep non-stick frying pan over high heat. Add
1 tablespoon of the fiery Sichuan oil, the white onion parts and the
garlic. Cook for 20–30 seconds. Add the gai lan and cooking wine
and cook for 2 minutes. Remove from the pan.

Add the noodles, the peanut soy sauce mixture and remaining
fiery Sichuan oil to taste and toss to combine. Cook for
8–10 minutes, tossing occasionally, until the noodles are crispy
and the sauce is reduced. Return the gai lan to the pan. Add the
peanuts and toss to combine.

Sprinkle with the remaining green onion, before serving. **SERVES 4**

Noodle Toppers

With a sprinkle of crunch and a drizzle of deliciousness, noodle bowls turn up a notch and explode with exciting new flavours and textures.

Thai-style cashew crunch

Place **2 stalks finely grated lemongrass (white part only)** and **4 finely shredded Thai lime leaves** in a small non-stick frying pan over medium heat. Cook for 3–4 minutes. Add **⅓ cup (50g) roughly chopped roasted salted cashews** and cook for 1 minute or until golden. Sprinkle with **1 teaspoon finely grated lime rind**.

SERVES 4 AS A TOPPING

Sichuan chilli oil

Place **¼ cup (60ml) grapeseed oil**, **1 tablespoon crushed Sichuan peppercorns** and **2 teaspoons dried chilli flakes** in a small saucepan over low heat. Cook for 2–3 minutes. Remove from the heat and allow to cool and infuse, before using.

SERVES 4 AS A TOPPING

garlic and green onion oil

Heat a small saucepan over medium-low heat. Add **¼ cup (60ml) grapeseed oil**, **6 cloves sliced garlic** and **4 sliced green onions (scallions) (white part only)** and cook for 5–6 minutes or until the garlic starts to colour. Remove from the heat and allow to cool and infuse, before using.

SERVES 4 AS A TOPPING

peanut chilli crunch

Place **2 chopped long red chillies, 2 tablespoons shredded ginger** and **¼ cup (60ml) grapeseed oil** in a small non-stick frying pan over medium-low heat. Cook for 6–7 minutes or until starting to colour. Add **⅓ cup (50g) roughly chopped roasted salted peanuts** and cook for 30 seconds or until heated through. **SERVES 4 AS A TOPPING**

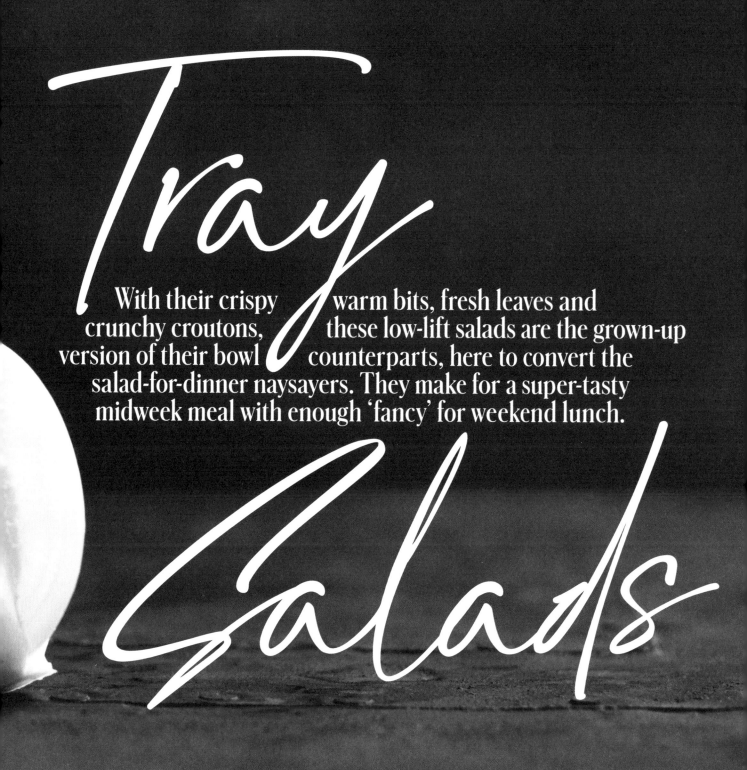

Tray

With their crispy crunchy croutons, version of their bowl warm bits, fresh leaves and these low-lift salads are the grown-up counterparts, here to convert the salad-for-dinner naysayers. They make for a super-tasty midweek meal with enough 'fancy' for weekend lunch.

Salads

sesame and miso chicken salad

2 eggwhites

2 tablespoons white miso paste

1 cup (160g) sesame seeds

4 x 180g chicken breast fillets, trimmed and cut into thirds

extra virgin olive oil, for drizzling

5 cups (400g) finely shredded wombok (Chinese cabbage)

1 cup (16g) coriander (cilantro) leaves

3 Lebanese cucumbers, sliced into ribbons using a
    vegetable peeler

2 green onions (scallions), thinly sliced

honey miso dressing

⅓ cup (120g) honey

⅓ cup (80ml) soy sauce

2 tablespoons white miso paste, extra

2 teaspoons sesame oil

TIP
I like to adopt
a freestyle
approach to the
herbs in this
salad, depending
on what I have
growing or at
home at the time.

Preheat oven grill (broiler) to high.

Whisk the eggwhites and miso together to combine. Place the sesame seeds in a shallow bowl.

Dip the chicken pieces into the miso eggwhites, then press both sides in the sesame seeds to coat.

Place on a baking tray lined with non-stick baking paper and drizzle with oil. Grill for 4–5 minutes each side or until golden.

While the chicken is grilling, make the honey miso dressing. Combine the honey, soy sauce, extra miso and sesame oil.

Place the wombok, coriander, cucumber, green onion and the honey miso dressing in a bowl and toss to combine.

Divide the salad between serving bowls and top with the sesame and miso chicken. **SERVES 4**

SCAN TO WATCH ME
CREATE THIS RECIPE

fennel, chorizo, grape and oregano salad

4 baby fennel bulbs, trimmed and quartered
250g red seedless grapes, cut into small bunches
16 sprigs oregano
560g chorizo (about 4), thickly sliced
extra virgin olive oil, for brushing
sea salt and cracked black pepper
100g wild leaf rocket (arugula)
200g blue cheese, broken into chunks
maple vinegar dressing
2 tablespoons red wine vinegar
2 tablespoons extra virgin olive oil
1 tablespoon pure maple syrup
½ teaspoon dried chilli flakes

TIP
Swap the blue cheese for a milder cheese, if you prefer.

Preheat oven to 220°C (440°F).

Place the fennel, grapes, oregano and chorizo on a baking tray lined with non-stick baking paper. Brush with oil and sprinkle with salt and pepper. Bake for 30–35 minutes.

While the chorizo and fennel are baking, make the maple vinegar dressing. Combine the red wine vinegar, oil, maple syrup and chilli.

Place the fennel, grapes and chorizo on a serving platter. Top with the rocket and blue cheese. Drizzle with the maple vinegar dressing, to serve. **SERVES 4**

BLAT salad

6 rashers bacon, trimmed and halved

400g large fresh sourdough chunks

300g cherry tomatoes, halved

2 tablespoons oregano leaves, chopped

2 tablespoons extra virgin olive oil

sea salt and cracked black pepper

2 baby cos (romaine) lettuces, trimmed and leaves separated

1 large avocado, deseeded and cut into quarters

creamy mustard dressing

¾ cup (180g) crème fraîche

2 teaspoons Dijon mustard

1 tablespoon lemon juice

TIP
I've reimagined the loved sandwich as a fresh, crunchy, creamy salad! Feel free to use gluten-free bread instead of sourdough.

Preheat oven to 200°C (400°F).

Place the bacon, sourdough, tomatoes, oregano, oil, salt and pepper in a bowl and gently toss to coat.

Place on a baking tray lined with non-stick baking paper and bake for 25 minutes or until golden.

To make the creamy mustard dressing, combine the crème fraîche, mustard and lemon juice.

Serve with the lettuce, avocado and creamy mustard dressing. Sprinkle with cracked black pepper. **SERVES 4**

toasted hazelnut, chickpea and apple salad

3 x 400g cans chickpeas (garbanzo beans), rinsed and drained
sea salt and cracked black pepper
1 cup (140g) hazelnuts, halved
3 heads witlof, trimmed and leaves separated
2 green apples, thinly sliced
2 cups (32g) mint leaves
200g firm feta
maple vinegar dressing
⅓ cup (80ml) pure maple syrup, plus 2 tablespoons extra
⅓ cup (80ml) apple cider vinegar
¼ cup (60ml) extra virgin olive oil

TIP
Swap the
witlof for
1 trimmed head
of radicchio,
if you like.

Preheat oven to 220°C (425°F).

To make the maple vinegar dressing, combine the maple syrup, apple cider vinegar and oil. Set aside.

Place the chickpeas, ¼ cup (60ml) of the dressing, the extra maple syrup, salt and pepper in a bowl and mix to combine.

Place on a large baking tray lined with non-stick baking paper and toast for 20 minutes.

Add the hazelnuts and toast for a further 10 minutes. Allow to cool.

To serve, place the witlof, apple, mint and feta on a serving platter. Top with the toasted chickpeas and hazelnuts and drizzle with the remaining dressing. **SERVES 4**

creamy potato, rocket and caper salad

1kg kipfler (fingerling) potatoes, halved lengthways
2 tablespoons rosemary leaves
2 tablespoons baby capers, rinsed and drained
1 head garlic, base trimmed
¼ cup (60ml) extra virgin olive oil
sea salt and cracked black pepper
⅓ cup (100g) whole-egg mayonnaise
⅓ cup (80g) sour cream
2 tablespoons chives, finely chopped
1 tablespoon white wine vinegar
2 cups (50g) wild baby rocket (arugula) leaves
1 bunch radish, trimmed and thinly sliced

TIP
If you can't find kipfler potatoes, use baby new potatoes instead.

Preheat oven to 220°C (440°F).

Place the potatoes, rosemary, capers, garlic, oil, salt and pepper in a bowl and toss to coat.

Place on a large baking tray lined with non-stick baking paper. Roast for 30 minutes or until golden.

Squeeze the roasted garlic into a bowl and mash until smooth. Add the mayonnaise, sour cream, chives, vinegar, salt and pepper and mix to combine.

To assemble, toss the rosemary potatoes and capers with the rocket and radish. Serve with the creamy garlic dressing. **SERVES 4**

Croutons

These moreish cubes will add salty crunch and body to just about any salad! They're a simple way to turn a side into a meal.

garlic and oregano croutons

Preheat oven to 200°C (400°F). Combine **360g fresh sourdough chunks, 6 cloves crushed garlic, 2 tablespoons oregano leaves, ⅓ cup (80ml) extra virgin olive oil, sea salt and cracked black pepper**. Place on a baking tray lined with non-stick baking paper. Bake for 10–12 minutes or until golden. **SERVES 4 AS A SALAD TOPPING**

wasabi croutons

Preheat oven to 180°C (350°F). Whisk
**2 tablespoons each of wasabi paste and hot
water, ⅓ cup (80ml) grapeseed oil, sea salt
and cracked black pepper** together. Add **360g
fresh sourdough chunks** and toss to combine.
Place on a baking tray lined with non-stick baking
paper. Bake for 10–12 minutes or until golden.
SERVES 4 AS A SALAD TOPPING

herb and parmesan croutons

Preheat oven to 200°C (400°F). Combine
**360g fresh sourdough chunks, ½ cup (40g)
finely grated parmesan, 2 tablespoons
rosemary leaves, ⅓ cup (80ml) extra virgin
olive oil, sea salt and cracked black pepper**.
Place on a baking tray lined with non-stick baking
paper. Bake for 10–12 minutes or until golden.
SERVES 4 AS A SALAD TOPPING

chilli croutons

Preheat oven to 200°C (400°F). Combine
**360g fresh sourdough chunks, 2 teaspoons
dried chilli flakes, ⅓ cup (80ml) grapeseed oil,
sea salt and cracked black pepper**. Place on
a baking tray lined with non-stick baking paper.
Bake for 10–12 minutes or until golden.
SERVES 4 AS A SALAD TOPPING

Rice

A handful of greens, some punchy proteins and a few clever flavour shortcuts create satisfying bowls overflowing with all of the good things, ready to step in as your weeknight saviour or weekend nourish bowl.

Bowls

sticky ginger chicken bowl

6 x 125g chicken thigh fillets, trimmed and cut into thirds
4 cups (560g) cooked quinoa
¼ cup (70g) store-bought pickled ginger, chopped
and 2 tablespoons pickled ginger liquid reserved
2 bok choy, halved and blanched
700g broccolini (sprouting broccoli), trimmed,
halved and blanched
thinly sliced green onion (scallion), shiso leaves and
extra store-bought pickled ginger, to serve
sticky ginger sauce
½ cup (125ml) pure maple syrup
¼ cup (60ml) soy sauce
2 tablespoons thinly sliced fresh ginger
3 cloves garlic, finely grated
2 tablespoons grapeseed oil, plus extra for drizzling
2 teaspoons sesame oil

Preheat oven to 220°C (440°F).

To make the sticky ginger sauce, combine the maple syrup, soy sauce, fresh ginger, garlic, grapeseed oil and sesame oil.

Place the sticky ginger sauce in a small saucepan over high heat. Cook for 4–5 minutes or until slightly thickened. Remove from the heat, add the chicken and mix to coat.

Place the chicken on a baking tray lined with non-stick baking paper and top with any remaining sticky ginger sauce. Drizzle with the extra oil and bake for 20–25 minutes or until golden and starting to caramelise.

Combine the quinoa, pickled ginger and pickled ginger liquid.

To assemble, divide the pickled ginger quinoa between bowls. Top with the sticky ginger chicken, bok choy, broccolini, green onion, shiso and the extra pickled ginger. **SERVES 4**

greens bowl with garlic quinoa

3 zucchinis (courgettes), shredded using a julienne peeler
1 avocado, deseeded and cut into quarters
400g snow peas (mange tout), blanched and halved
300g labne or soft feta
⅓ cup (55g) toasted pepitas (pumpkin seeds), chopped
lemon wedges and extra virgin olive oil or green goddess
   yoghurt dressing (see *recipe*, page 172), to serve
garlic and kale quinoa
2 tablespoons extra virgin olive oil
4 cloves garlic, sliced
5 cups (700g) cooked quinoa
⅓ cup (6g) dill leaves, chopped
sea salt and cracked black pepper
4 stalks kale, stems removed, roughly chopped and blanched

TIP
If you don't have a julienne peeler, use a vegetable peeler to create zucchini ribbons instead.

To make the garlic and kale quinoa, heat a large frying pan over medium heat.

Add the oil and garlic and cook for 1–2 minutes or until soft. Add the quinoa, dill, salt and pepper and toss to warm through. Add the kale and toss to combine.

To assemble, divide the garlic and kale quinoa between serving bowls. Top with the zucchini, avocado, snow peas, labne and pepitas.

Serve with a squeeze of lemon and a drizzle of oil, or the green goddess yoghurt dressing. **SERVES 4**

 SCAN TO WATCH ME CREATE THIS RECIPE

chipotle salmon and black rice bowl

5 cups (1kg) cooked black rice

400g cherry tomatoes, cut in half

1 avocado, deseeded and chopped

½ red onion, thinly sliced

coriander (cilantro), to serve

chipotle salmon

⅓ cup (80g) chipotle chillies in adobo sauce+, finely chopped

2 tablespoons extra virgin olive oil

4 x 170g skinless salmon fillets, cut into thirds

zingy dressing

1 teaspoon smoked paprika

¼ cup (60ml) extra virgin olive oil

2 teaspoons honey

1 tablespoon lime juice

TIP
Feel free to use brown rice instead of black rice.

Preheat oven grill (broiler) to high.

To make the chipotle salmon, combine the chipotle chillies and the oil in a bowl. Add the salmon and gently mix to coat.

Place the salmon on a baking tray lined with non-stick baking paper. Grill for 3–4 minutes or until cooked to your liking.

To make the zingy dressing, whisk the paprika, oil, honey and lime juice together to combine.

To assemble, divide the rice between serving bowls. Top with the chipotle salmon, cherry tomatoes, avocado, red onion and coriander. Drizzle with the zingy dressing, to serve. **SERVES 4**

+ *Chipotle chilli in adobo sauce is available at most supermarkets or at specialty stores.*

dukkah-spiced egg bowl

¼ cup (30g) dukkah
4 soft-boiled eggs
5 cups (825g) cooked brown rice
16 spears asparagus, trimmed and blanched
400g green beans, trimmed and blanched
1 tablespoon tarragon leaves, extra
2 teaspoons finely grated lemon rind, extra
2 bagels or baguettes, thinly sliced and toasted, to serve
tarragon yoghurt dressing
1 cup (250g) plain thick yoghurt
2 tablespoons chopped tarragon leaves
1 teaspoon finely grated lemon rind
sea salt and cracked black pepper

TIP
If you don't have dukkah at home, combine toasted sesame seeds with sea salt flakes and spices such as cumin and coriander instead.

To make the tarragon yoghurt dressing, combine the yoghurt, chopped tarragon, lemon rind, salt and pepper. Set aside.

Place the dukkah in a bowl. Add the eggs, one at a time, gently rolling to coat them in the dukkah.

To assemble, divide the rice, asparagus and green beans between serving bowls. Top with the dukkah-coated egg, extra tarragon and tarragon yoghurt dressing. Sprinkle with the extra lemon rind and serve with the toasted bagels. SERVES 4

cauliflower kimchi bowl

800g cauliflower florets
450g firm tofu, drained and sliced into strips
5 cups (825g) cooked brown rice
800g gai lan (Chinese broccoli), trimmed and blanched
1 cup (280g) chopped kimchi
coriander (cilantro) and thinly sliced long green chilli, to serve
spiced honey dressing
⅓ cup (100g) gochujang⁺ (Korean chilli paste)
¼ cup (60ml) water
2 tablespoons honey
2 tablespoons extra virgin olive oil

TIP
If you can't find kimchi, mix a little sauerkraut with chilli sauce to make a cheat's substitute.

Preheat oven to 220°C (440°F).

To make the spiced honey dressing, combine the gochujang, water, honey and oil in a large bowl.

Add the cauliflower and tofu and toss to coat. Place on a large baking tray lined with non-stick baking paper. Bake for 35 minutes or until golden.

To assemble, divide the rice and gai lan between serving bowls. Top with the kimchi, spiced honey cauliflower and tofu, coriander and chilli. **SERVES 4**

+ *Find gochujang in select supermarkets and Asian grocers.*
If you can't find it, use any other mild chilli paste.

Salad Toppers

Snoozy salads transform into rocking rice bowls with these extra flavour kicks, turning each mouthful into a crunchy, zingy flavour party.

tahini dressing

Whisk **½ cup (140g) hulled tahini**, **⅓ cup (80ml) lemon juice**, **1 tablespoon honey** and **⅓ cup (125ml) water** together, adding **more water** if needed. Sprinkle with **sumac, to serve**. **MAKES 1⅓ CUPS**

green goddess yoghurt dressing

Place **1 cup (250g) plain thick yoghurt**, **1 cup (24g) flat-leaf parsley leaves**, **1 cup (16g) mint leaves**, **½ cup (8g) coriander leaves**, **3 chopped green onions (scallions)**, **1 deseeded and roughly chopped avocado**, **½ cup (125ml) water**, **⅓ cup (80ml) lemon juice**, **sea salt and cracked black pepper** in a blender and blend until smooth. **MAKES 2½ CUPS**

crunchy seed sprinkle

Heat a large non-stick frying pan over medium heat. Add **⅓ cup (55g) each of pepitas (pumpkin seeds) and sunflower seeds, 2 tablespoons sesame seeds, ⅓ cup (80ml) pure maple syrup** and **sea salt flakes** and mix to combine. Cook for 5–6 minutes, stirring occasionally, until the seeds are lightly golden and the syrup is reduced. Spoon onto a baking tray lined with non-stick baking paper and allow to cool. Break into chunks and store in an airtight container for up to 1 week. **MAKES 1 CUP**

chilli ginger cashew sprinkle

Heat a large non-stick frying pan over medium heat. Add **1½ cups (225g) raw unsalted cashews, 3 dried chillies that have been deseeded and sliced, 1 tablespoon shredded ginger** and **⅓ cup (120g) honey** and mix to combine. Cook for 5–6 minutes, stirring occasionally, until the cashews are golden and the honey is reduced. Spoon onto a baking tray lined with non-stick baking paper and allow to cool. Break into chunks and store in an airtight container for up to 1 week. **MAKES 2 CUPS**

Sweet

Flourless

I love the fudgy centres and bronzed tops you're gifted when you bake with almond meal! Rich, moist and decadent, these flourless versions of your favourites also happen to be bursting with better-for-you ingredients.

Cakes

chocolate truffle cake

6 eggs
½ cup (125ml) pure maple syrup
1¼ cups (300g) firmly packed brown sugar
1 cup (100g) cocoa, plus extra for dusting
1½ cups (180g) almond meal (ground almonds)
½ cup (125ml) grapeseed oil

TIP
Store any
leftover cake
in an airtight
container in a
cool dry place.

Preheat oven to 160°C (325°F). Line a 24cm (9½ inch) round
springform cake tin with non-stick baking paper.

Place the eggs, maple syrup and sugar into the bowl of an
electric mixer and whisk on high speed for 10 minutes or until
light and fluffy.

Sift the cocoa and almond meal over and gently fold to combine.
Add the oil and fold to combine.

Pour the mixture into the prepared tin and bake for
35–40 minutes or until the cake is firm around the edges but has
a slight wobble in the centre. Allow to cool slightly, then refrigerate
for 1 hour or until set.

Remove the cake from the tin and place on a cake stand or
serving plate. Dust with extra cocoa, to serve. **SERVES 10-12**

SCAN TO WATCH ME
CREATE THIS RECIPE

banana coconut dream cake

2 eggs

1½ cups (390g) mashed banana

¾ cup (180ml) light-flavoured extra virgin olive oil

1 cup (250g) plain thick yoghurt

1 cup (240g) firmly packed brown sugar

2 cups (160g) desiccated coconut

1 cup (120g) almond meal (ground almonds)

½ cup (80g) rice flour

3 teaspoons baking powder

yoghurt frosting (see *recipe*, page 189) and toasted coconut
   flakes, to serve

TIP
This cake is
just as delicious
with or without
the frosting.

Preheat oven to 160°C (325°F). Line a 20cm x 30cm (8 inch x
12 inch) slice tin with non-stick baking paper.

   Place the eggs, banana, oil, yoghurt and sugar in a bowl and
whisk to combine. Add the coconut, almond meal, rice flour
and baking powder and whisk to combine.

   Pour the mixture into the prepared tin and bake for
45–50 minutes or until cooked when tested with a skewer.
Allow to cool in the tin for 10 minutes, before turning out onto
a wire rack to cool completely.

   Place the cake on a serving plate. Top with the yoghurt frosting
and sprinkle with coconut flakes, to serve. **SERVES 12**

SCAN TO WATCH ME
CREATE THIS RECIPE

pistachio sponge cake with rose cream

4 eggs
½ cup (110g) caster (superfine) sugar
2 teaspoons rosewater
¾ cup (105g) ground pistachios[+]
1 cup (120g) almond meal (ground almonds)
2½ tablespoons cornflour (cornstarch)
edible rose petals[++], extra ground pistachios and rose cream
  (see *recipe*, page 189), to serve

TIP
You could also scatter some fresh raspberries over this cake to serve.

Preheat oven to 160°C (325°F). Line the base of a 20cm (8 inch) round cake tin with non-stick baking paper and lightly grease the sides.

Place the eggs, sugar and rosewater in the bowl of an electric mixer and whisk on high speed for 8 minutes or until thick and doubled in volume.

In a separate bowl, combine ½ cup of the ground pistachios, the almond meal and cornflour. Add the pistachio mixture to the egg mixture and gently fold to combine, using a metal spoon.

Pour the mixture into the prepared tin and bake for 25–30 minutes or until the cake starts to come away from the tin. Allow to cool in the tin for 20 minutes, before turning out onto a wire rack to cool completely.

Place the cake on a cake stand or plate. Top with rose petals and the remaining ground pistachios. Serve with rose cream. **SERVES 10**

+ *To make enough ground pistachios for this recipe, place ¾ cup (105g) whole unsalted pistachios in a small food processor and process until finely chopped.*

++ *Find edible rose petals at select supermarkets or specialty food stores.*

Earl Grey, lemon and blueberry cake

1 tablespoon Earl Grey tea leaves
¼ cup (60ml) milk
4 eggs
2 eggwhites
1 tablespoon finely grated lemon rind
1 cup (220g) raw caster (superfine) sugar
3 cups (360g) almond meal (ground almonds)
3 teaspoons baking powder
1 cup (125g) blueberries
yoghurt frosting (see *recipe*, page 189), to serve

TIP
This cake is just as delicious served warm without the frosting.

Preheat oven to 160°C (325°F). Line a 10cm x 24cm (4 inch x 9½ inch) loaf tin with non-stick baking paper.

Place the tea leaves and milk in a small saucepan over medium heat. Bring to a gentle simmer, then remove from the heat and allow to infuse for 10 minutes. Strain and reserve the milk. Discard the tea leaves.

Place the infused milk, eggs, eggwhites, lemon rind, sugar, almond meal and baking powder in a large bowl and whisk to combine. Add the blueberries and fold through.

Pour the mixture into the prepared tin and bake for 45 minutes or until golden and cooked when tested with a skewer. Allow to cool in the tin for 10 minutes, before turning out onto a wire rack to cool completely.

Place the cake on a serving plate and top with the yoghurt frosting, to serve. **SERVES 12**

caramel mud cake

2 eggs
1⅓ cups (335g) plain thick yoghurt
⅓ cup (80ml) grapeseed oil
1 tablespoon vanilla extract
1¼ cups (185g) coconut sugar
¼ cup (55g) raw caster (superfine) sugar
1½ cups (180g) almond meal (ground almonds)
½ cup (80g) buckwheat flour
2 teaspoons baking powder
coconut caramel sauce (see *recipe*, page 188), to serve

TIP
To grease a
bundt tin,
brush it with
melted butter
and refrigerate
until the
butter is set.

Preheat oven to 160°C (325°F). Lightly grease a 3-litre-capacity bundt tin.

Place the eggs, yoghurt, oil, vanilla, coconut sugar and raw caster sugar in a bowl and whisk together until smooth.

Add the almond meal, buckwheat flour and baking powder and whisk to combine.

Pour the mixture into the prepared tin and bake for 35 minutes or until cooked when tested with a skewer. Allow to cool in the tin for 10 minutes, before gently turning out onto a wire rack to cool completely.

Place the cake on a cake stand or plate and drizzle with coconut caramel sauce, to serve. **SERVES 10-12**

SCAN TO WATCH ME
CREATE THIS RECIPE

Frosting

Enriched with nice-for-you stuff, these glossy crowns add a tasty layer of wow to any baked treat. Just grab your favourite spatula and slather up!

coconut caramel sauce

Place **1 cup (250ml) coconut cream**, **¾ cup (110g) coconut sugar** and **1 teaspoon vanilla extract** in a large non-stick frying pan over high heat and cook for 2 minutes, stirring, until the sugar dissolves and the mixture is boiling. Cook the caramel over medium-high heat, stirring occasionally, paying close attention as it can stick to the bottom of the pan. Continue stirring for 6 minutes or until it has thickened. It should leave a trail when you run your spoon or spatula through it. Allow to cool slightly, before pouring into sterilised jars or clean glass storage containers. **MAKES 200ML**

chocolate frosting

Place **300g chopped dark (70% cocoa) chocolate** in a heatproof bowl over a saucepan of simmering water (the bowl shouldn't touch the water) and stir until melted and smooth. Remove from the heat, add **¾ cup (180ml) pure cream** and **150g sour cream** and stir to combine.
MAKES 2¼ CUPS

rose cream

Place **1 cup (250ml) pure cream** in a bowl and whip until soft peaks form. Add **1 teaspoon rosewater** and sift in **¼ cup (40g) icing (confectioner's) sugar**. Whisk to combine.
MAKES 1¼ CUPS

yoghurt frosting

Place **1 cup (250g) mascarpone, 1 cup (250g) plain thick yoghurt, 1 tablespoon honey** and **1 teaspoon vanilla extract** in a bowl and whisk until thick and fluffy. **MAKES 2 CUPS**

Better For You Treats

What if you could enjoy those delicious treats you love – but with more balance and fabulous flavour thanks to some simple switch-ups? These chewy, creamy morsels are just the answer when the clock strikes sweet o'clock.

raspberry choc coconut slice

60g dark (70% cocoa) chocolate, chopped
coconut base
1 cup (150g) unsalted cashews
1 cup (80g) desiccated coconut
¼ cup (60ml) light agave or pure maple syrup
raspberry filling
3 cups (375g) frozen raspberries, thawed
2 tablespoons light agave or pure maple syrup, extra
1 cup (80g) desiccated coconut, extra
6 soft fresh dates (about 120g), pitted
2 teaspoons vanilla extract

TIP
Store the slice in an airtight container in the refrigerator for up to a week.

To make the coconut base, line a 20cm (8 inch) square slice tin with non-stick baking paper.

Place the cashews, coconut and agave in a food processor and process for 1–2 minutes, scraping down the sides of the bowl, until the mixture comes together. Press the mixture firmly into the prepared tin, using the back of a spoon. Refrigerate for 30 minutes or until set.

To make the raspberry filling, place the raspberries into a sieve over a bowl. Using a spoon, press the raspberries to remove the seeds. Discard the seeds.

Heat a non-stick frying pan over medium heat. Add the raspberries and extra agave and cook for 8–10 minutes or until the mixture has reduced and you can run your spoon or spatula through it.

Place the extra coconut, dates and vanilla in the clean bowl of a food processor and process for 1 minute or until just combined. Add the raspberries and process for 30 seconds or until just combined. Pour the raspberry filling over the coconut base, spreading it out evenly. Refrigerate for 30 minutes or until firm. Slice into bars and place on a baking tray lined with non-stick baking paper.

Place the chocolate in a heatproof bowl over a saucepan of simmering water (the bowl shouldn't touch the water) and stir until melted.

Drizzle the melted chocolate over the slice. Refrigerate for 1 hour or until set, before serving. **MAKES 10**

no-fuss
choc chunk cookies

1 cup (250g) cashew butter
½ cup (75g) coconut sugar
⅓ cup (75g) raw caster (superfine) sugar
1 egg
1 tablespoon vanilla extract
1½ cups (135g) rolled oats
100g dark (70% cocoa) chocolate, chopped

TIP
For a nutty twist, add a handful of chopped walnuts, almonds or macadamias.

Preheat oven to 180°C (350°F).

Combine the cashew butter, coconut sugar, caster sugar, egg and vanilla in a bowl.

Add the oats and chocolate and mix to combine.

Divide the dough into 8 portions and roll into balls. Place on a large baking tray lined with non-stick baking paper.

Bake for 13 minutes or until lightly golden. Allow to cool on the tray. **MAKES 8**

choc caramel fudge

16 soft fresh dates (about 320g), pitted
⅓ cup (80g) cashew butter or hulled tahini
2 teaspoons vanilla bean paste
1 teaspoon sea salt flakes (optional), to serve
chocolate topping
100g dark (70% cocoa) chocolate, chopped
⅛ teaspoon grapeseed oil

TIP
This fudge is best eaten almost straight from the freezer, or store it in an airtight container in the freezer for up to 2 weeks.

Line a 10cm x 20cm (4 inch x 8 inch) loaf tin with non-stick baking paper.

Place the dates, cashew butter and vanilla in a food processor and process for 2–3 minutes or until the mixture is smooth and comes together.

Press into the prepared tin and smooth the surface, using the back of a spoon. Freeze for 20 minutes or until very cold.

To make the chocolate topping, place the chocolate in a heatproof bowl over a saucepan of simmering water (the bowl shouldn't touch the water) and stir until melted. Add the oil and stir to combine.

Pour the chocolate over the fudge and sprinkle with salt, if desired. Freeze for 30 minutes or until set.

Cut the fudge into bars, to serve. **MAKES 12**

coconut crème brûlée

2 cups (250g) frozen raspberries
¼ cup (60ml) water
⅓ cup (80ml) pure maple syrup
1 x 400ml can coconut cream
¼ cup (50g) white chia seeds
2 teaspoons vanilla bean paste
1½ tablespoons raw caster (superfine) sugar

TIP
You could also use the chia jams (*pages 232–233*) as your fruity base for these brûlées.

Place the raspberries, water and ¼ cup (60ml) of the maple syrup in a medium saucepan over high heat. Cook, stirring occasionally, for 10–12 minutes or until thickened. Set aside for 15 minutes to cool.

While the raspberry mixture is cooling, place the coconut cream, chia seeds, vanilla and remaining maple syrup in a blender and blend for 1 minute.

Divide the raspberry mixture between 4 x 1½-cup (375ml) capacity ramekins. Top with the coconut chia mixture and refrigerate for 2–4 hours or until set.

Sprinkle with the caster sugar and, using a kitchen blowtorch, caramelise the sugar. **SERVES 4**

chia jam drop cookies

2 cups (320g) buckwheat flour
1½ cups (180g) almond meal (ground almonds)
1 teaspoon ground cinnamon
¾ cup (180ml) pure maple syrup
½ cup (125ml) grapeseed oil
⅓ cup (95g) fruity chia jam (see *recipes*, pages 232–233) or
store-bought jam

Preheat oven to 180°C (350°F). Line 2 baking trays with non-stick baking paper.

Place the flour, almond meal, cinnamon, maple syrup and oil in a bowl and mix to combine.

Roll heaped tablespoonfuls of the mixture into balls and place on the prepared trays, allowing a little room to spread. Press your thumb gently into the middle of each cookie to make an indent. Fill with 1 heaped teaspoon of the chia jam.

Bake for 16–18 minutes or until golden and crisp. **MAKES 20**

Smoothies

Your favourite dessert flavour combos have been blended into speedy smoothies to create fresh and frosty drinkable snacks or brekky treats.

salted caramel smoothie

Place **4 soft fresh pitted dates (about 80g)** in a heatproof bowl and cover with **boiling water**. Allow to stand for 10 minutes or until softened, then drain. Place the softened dates, **2½ tablespoons coconut sugar**, **2 cups (500ml) almond or coconut milk**, **2 tablespoons cashew butter** and **2 cups ice cubes** in a blender and blend until smooth. Pour into 2 chilled serving glasses and sprinkle with **sea salt flakes**. SERVES 2

lime, passionfruit and coconut smoothie

Place **2 cups (500ml) coconut milk**, **⅓ cup (80ml) lime juice**, **2 tablespoons light agave syrup** and **2 cups ice cubes** in a blender and blend until smooth. Pour into 2 chilled serving glasses and top with **fresh passionfruit pulp** and **finely grated lime rind**. SERVES 2

strawberry crush smoothie

Place **2 cups (250g) strawberries**, **1 tablespoon honey** and **1 teaspoon rosewater** in a blender and blend until smooth. Pour into the base of 2 chilled serving glasses and swirl to coat. Place **2 cups (500ml) chilled milk**, **1 cup (250g) plain thick yoghurt** and **2 cups ice cubes** in the cleaned blender and blend until smooth. Pour over the strawberry swirl and stir, to serve. **SERVES 2**

choc espresso smoothie

Combine **2 tablespoons each of cocoa and pure maple syrup** until smooth. Spoon into the base of 2 chilled serving glasses and swirl to coat. Place **2 cups (500ml) chilled almond milk**, **⅓ cup (80ml) espresso coffee**, **6 soft fresh pitted and halved dates (about 120g)**, **2 tablespoons cashew butter** and **2 cups ice cubes** in a blender and blend until smooth. Pour over the cocoa swirl and stir, to serve. **SERVES 2**

Fruity

I love filling the house with the scent of sticky fruits baking into super soft, spiced-up baked treats! Even better when there's a bounty of wholesome seeds, flours and plant-based swap-ins to sweeten the deal.

Desserts

banoffee brûlée tarts

1 cup (120g) almond meal (ground almonds)
1 cup (100g) flaked almonds
2 eggwhites
¼ cup (55g) raw caster (superfine) sugar
2 bananas, peeled and thinly sliced
¼ cup (35g) coconut sugar
coconut caramel sauce (see *recipe*, page 188), to serve
whipped vanilla cream
½ cup (125g) mascarpone
½ cup (125g) plain thick yoghurt
1 teaspoon vanilla bean paste or vanilla extract

TIP
If you don't own a kitchen blowtorch, use the grill in your oven (broiler) to caramelise the banana.

Preheat oven to 180°C (350°F). Line a large baking tray with non-stick baking paper.

Place the almond meal, flaked almonds, eggwhites and the caster sugar in a bowl and mix to combine. Divide the mixture into 4. Place on the prepared tray and press out into rough 12cm (4¾ inch) rounds. Bake for 14 minutes or until golden around the edges.

To make the whipped vanilla cream, whisk the mascarpone, yoghurt and vanilla until soft peaks form.

Place the banana slices on a baking tray lined with non-stick baking paper and sprinkle with the coconut sugar. Using a kitchen blowtorch, cook until the banana starts to caramelise.

To assemble, divide the whipped vanilla cream between tart bases. Top with the coconut caramel sauce and the caramelised banana. **SERVES 4**

SCAN TO WATCH ME
CREATE THIS RECIPE

pear ricotta cake

6 small firm pears, peeled
1 cup (220g) raw caster (superfine) sugar
2 cinnamon sticks
1 litre water
ground cinnamon and icing (confectioner's) sugar, for dusting
ricotta cake
6 eggs
¾ cup (165g) raw caster (superfine) sugar
500g fresh ricotta
1½ cups (180g) almond meal (ground almonds)
¼ cup (35g) cornflour (cornstarch)
1 teaspoon baking powder
1 teaspoon ground cinnamon
2 teaspoons vanilla extract

TIP
This cake is
delicious served
either warm
or cold.

Place the pears, sugar, cinnamon and water in a large saucepan over medium heat. Cook for 10 minutes or until the pears start to soften. Remove the pears from the pan and set aside to cool.

To make the ricotta cake, whisk the eggs and sugar together until combined. Add the ricotta and fold through to combine. Add the almond meal, cornflour, baking powder, cinnamon and vanilla and whisk to combine.

Pour the mixture into a 24cm (9½ inch) round springform cake tin lined with non-stick baking paper. Arrange the pears over the mixture, nestling them in slightly to secure.

Bake for 1 hour and 10 minutes or until cooked when tested with a skewer. Allow to cool slightly in the tin.

Remove the cake from the tin and place on a cake stand or plate. Dust with cinnamon and icing sugar, to serve. **SERVES 10-12**

fig and coconut tart

1 cup (150g) plain wholemeal (whole-wheat) flour
½ cup (75g) plain (all purpose) flour
¼ cup (55g) caster (superfine) sugar
125g very cold unsalted butter
¼ cup (60ml) iced water
1 teaspoon vanilla extract
7 figs, sliced into thirds
1½ tablespoons demerara sugar
vanilla bean ice-cream or yoghurt, to serve
coconut filling
⅓ cup (25g) desiccated coconut
1 teaspoon finely grated orange rind
¼ cup (55g) caster (superfine) sugar, extra

TIP
Swap the figs
for thinly sliced
apples, pears,
fresh berries
or summer
stone fruits.

Place the flours and the sugar in a bowl. Using a box grater, grate the butter into the flour mixture. Add the iced water and vanilla and, using your fingertips, mix until a soft dough forms.

Roll out the pastry between sheets of non-stick baking paper to a rough 24cm x 36cm (9½ inch x 14 inch) oval shape. Place on a baking tray and refrigerate until firm.

Preheat oven to 200°C (400°F).

To make the coconut filling, place the coconut, orange rind and extra sugar in a bowl and mix to combine.

Remove the top sheet of baking paper. Sprinkle the coconut filling over the pastry, leaving a 5cm border.

Top with the figs and fold the excess pastry over to form an edge. Sprinkle the figs and pastry with the demerara sugar.

Bake for 35–40 minutes or until the pastry is crisp and golden. Serve the tart warm or cold with vanilla bean ice-cream or yoghurt. **SERVES 8**

apple crumble parfait

vanilla bean ice-cream, vanilla bean yoghurt or
  frozen yoghurt, to serve
crumble topping
1 cup (90g) rolled oats
1 cup (100g) flaked almonds
2 eggwhites
⅓ cup (75g) raw caster (superfine) sugar
spiced apple
3 green apples, cored and cut into cubes
1½ teaspoons ground cinnamon
1 tablespoon pure maple syrup
1 teaspoon vanilla bean paste

TIP
For an even speedier dessert, make the crumble topping ahead of time and store it in an airtight container.

Preheat oven to 180°C (350°F).

To make the crumble topping, combine the oats, almonds, eggwhites and sugar. Place on a baking tray lined with non-stick baking paper. Bake for 10–15 minutes or until crisp and golden.

To make the spiced apple, combine the apple, cinnamon, maple syrup and vanilla.

To assemble, divide the spiced apple between serving glasses and top with ice-cream or yoghurt and the crumble topping. **SERVES 4**

rhubarb and raspberry slice

500g chopped rhubarb (about 5 stalks)
2 cups (250g) raspberries
⅓ cup (75g) raw caster (superfine) sugar
2 tablespoons cornflour (cornstarch)
2 teaspoons vanilla extract
vanilla cinnamon yoghurt (see *recipe*, page 248),
   to serve (optional)
oaty base
1 cup (90g) rolled oats
1 cup (120g) almond meal (ground almonds)
⅔ cup (65g) chopped walnuts
8 soft fresh dates (about 160g), pitted
1 teaspoon ground cinnamon
¼ cup (60ml) pure maple syrup

Preheat oven to 160°C (325°F). Line a 20cm x 30cm (8 inch x 12 inch) slice tin with non-stick baking paper.

To make the oaty base, place the oats, almond meal, walnuts, dates, cinnamon and maple syrup in a food processor and process until finely chopped.

Press the mixture firmly into the prepared tin and bake for 20 minutes or until golden.

Place the rhubarb, raspberries, sugar, cornflour and vanilla in a bowl and toss to coat.

Top the oaty base with the rhubarb mixture and bake for a further 45–50 minutes or until the rhubarb is soft. Allow to cool in the tin for 10 minutes.

Serve warm or cold with vanilla cinnamon yoghurt, if desired.

SERVES 8–10

Popsicles

These creamy pops of yum are a super fun way to finish a meal! They're an easy make-ahead dessert or sweet snack to have on stand-by in the freezer.

yoghurt pop base

Place **1⅓ cups (330g) plain thick yoghurt**, **¼ cup (55g) caster (superfine) sugar** and **2 teaspoons vanilla extract** in a bowl and mix to combine. Divide between 8 x ⅓-cup (80ml) popsicle moulds. Top with a spoonful of your **chosen fruit mixture** (see *recipes*, below and right) and swirl through. Insert popsicle sticks and freeze for 4–6 hours or until firm. **MAKES 8**

banana cinnamon pops

Place **2 small ripe mashed bananas**, **2 tablespoons caster (superfine) sugar** and **½ teaspoon ground cinnamon** in a bowl and mash together to combine. Spoon over the **yoghurt pop base** (see *recipe*, above) and swirl through. Insert popsicle sticks and freeze for 4–6 hours or until firm. **MAKES 8**

218

passionfruit pops

Place ⅔ cup (80g) fresh passionfruit pulp, 2 teaspoons finely grated lime rind and 2 tablespoons caster (superfine) sugar in a bowl and mash together to combine. Spoon over the yoghurt pop base (see *recipe*, left) and swirl through. Insert popsicle sticks and freeze for 4–6 hours or until firm. MAKES 8

raspberry swirl pops

Place 1½ cups (185g) frozen and thawed raspberries and 2 tablespoons caster (superfine) sugar in a bowl and mash together to combine. Spoon over the yoghurt pop base (see *recipe*, left) and swirl through. Insert popsicle sticks and freeze for 4–6 hours or until firm. MAKES 8

mango pops

Place ⅔ cup (160ml) fresh mango purée and 2 tablespoons caster (superfine) sugar in a bowl and mash together to combine. Spoon over the yoghurt pop base (see *recipe*, left) and swirl through. Insert popsicle sticks and freeze for 4–6 hours or until firm. MAKES 8

Icy Treats

If I can have dessert frozen and ready to whip out at the meal's end, it makes for an even sweeter finish. Featuring classic crowd-pleasing flavour combos, these creamy no-churn delights will please big and little kids alike.

tiramisu ice-cream

750g fresh ricotta
1 cup (220g) raw caster (superfine) sugar
1 tablespoon vanilla extract
2 cups (500ml) pure cream
10 store-bought sponge finger biscuits (savoiardi),
  cut into quarters
espresso dip
⅓ cup (80ml) hot espresso coffee
¼ cup (60ml) pure maple syrup
¼ cup (25g) cocoa, plus extra for dusting

TIP
Using a
metal tin speeds
up the freezing
process.

Place the ricotta, sugar and vanilla in a food processor and process
until smooth.

Place the cream in a bowl and whisk until soft peaks form.

Add the cream to the ricotta mixture and fold through.

To make the espresso dip, combine the espresso, maple syrup
and cocoa.

Dip the biscuits into the espresso dip for 2 seconds.

Pour one third of the ricotta mixture into a 2.5 litre capacity
metal tin. Top with half the biscuits and another third of the ricotta
mixture. Repeat the layers, finishing with the ricotta mixture, and
smooth the top.

Freeze for 4–6 hours or until set. Dust the extra cocoa over,
to serve. **SERVES 6-8**

cashew coffee popsicles

1 cup (250g) cashew butter
1 cup (250ml) almond milk
⅓ cup (80ml) pure maple syrup
⅓ cup (80ml) espresso coffee
pinch of salt
60g dark (70% cocoa) chocolate, melted and cooled (optional)

TIP
Use any other milk you like for these popsicles.

Place the cashew butter, almond milk, maple syrup, espresso and salt in a blender and blend until smooth.

Divide the mixture between 6 x 100ml popsicle moulds. Insert popsicle sticks and freeze for 2–3 hours or until set.

For choc-drizzled popsicles, place them on a baking tray lined with non-stick baking paper and drizzle with the melted and cooled chocolate. **MAKES 6**

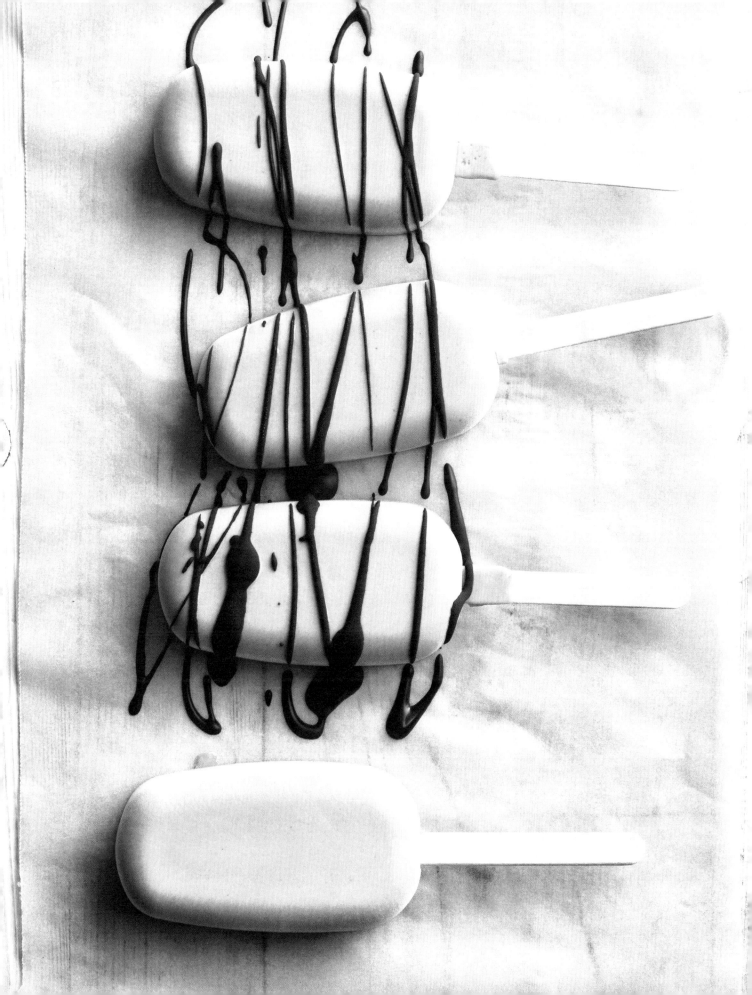

cheat's fro-yo

1kg plain thick yoghurt
2 tablespoons vanilla extract
½ cup (110g) raw caster (superfine) sugar
raspberry or passionfruit chia jam (see *recipes*,
**   pages 232–233), to serve**

TIP
Using small ice
cube trays will
make for a faster
freeze time.

Mix the yoghurt, vanilla and sugar in a large jug to combine.
  Pour into ice cube trays and freeze for 2–3 hours or until set.
  Remove the frozen yoghurt from the ice cube trays. Working in
2 batches, place in a food processor and process for 1–2 minutes
or until smooth.
  To assemble, layer the fro-yo and chia jam in glasses and serve.
SERVES 6

tangy lemon and ricotta cheesecake ice-cream

500g fresh ricotta
250g cream cheese, softened
1 cup (220g) raw caster (superfine) sugar
2 tablespoons finely grated lemon rind
½ cup (125ml) lemon juice
1½ cups (375ml) pure cream

Place the ricotta, cream cheese, sugar, lemon rind and juice in a food processor and process until smooth.

Place the cream in a bowl and whisk until soft peaks form.

Add the cream to the ricotta mixture and fold through. Pour into a 1.8 litre capacity metal tin and smooth the top.

Freeze for 4–6 hours or until set. **SERVES 6–8**

watermelon instant sorbet

950g watermelon pieces
¼ cup (60ml) light agave syrup

Layer the watermelon pieces in a freeze-proof container between sheets of non-stick baking paper. Freeze for 4 hours or overnight.

Place the frozen watermelon and the agave in a food processor and process for 3–5 minutes or until smooth.

Scoop into bowls or pour into a 20cm x 30cm (8 inch x 12 inch) freeze-proof container and freeze for 3–4 hours or until set.

SERVES 4

pineapple and mint instant sorbet

750g pineapple pieces
¼ cup (4g) mint leaves

TIP
For a fruity variation, swap 750g pineapple for banana and add a splash of vanilla.

Layer the pineapple pieces in a freeze-proof container between sheets of non-stick baking paper. Freeze for 4 hours or overnight.

Place the frozen pineapple and the mint in a food processor and process for 3–5 minutes or until smooth.

Scoop into bowls or pour into a 20cm x 30cm (8 inch x 12 inch) freeze-proof container and freeze for 3–4 hours or until set.

SERVES 4

Chia Jams

You favourite fruity preserves have been upflavoured and nutritionally upscaled thanks to a sprinkle of superstar chia seeds.

rhubarb and vanilla chia jam

Place **3 cups (360g) chopped rhubarb (about 4 stalks)**, **½ cup (110g) raw caster (superfine) sugar**, **½ cup (125ml) water** and **1 teaspoon vanilla extract** in a non-stick frying pan over medium-high heat. Cook for 15 minutes or until the rhubarb has softened. Remove from the heat. Add **2 tablespoons white chia seeds** and stir to combine. Allow to stand for 30 minutes or until thickened. Transfer to an airtight container and refrigerate until cool. **MAKES 1¾ CUPS**

blueberry chia jam

Place **2 cups (250g) frozen blueberries**, **¼ cup (55g) raw caster (superfine) sugar** and **¼ cup (60ml) water** in a non-stick frying pan over medium-high heat. Cook for 15 minutes or until the blueberries have softened. Remove from the heat. Add **2 tablespoons white chia seeds** and stir to combine. Allow to stand for 30 minutes or until thickened. Transfer to an airtight container and refrigerate until cool. **MAKES 1¼ CUPS**

raspberry chia jam

Place **2 cups (250g) frozen raspberries**, **¼ cup (55g) raw caster (superfine) sugar** and **¼ cup (60ml) water** in a non-stick frying pan over medium-high heat. Cook for 15 minutes or until the raspberries have softened. Remove from the heat. Add **2 tablespoons white chia seeds** and stir to combine. Allow to stand for 30 minutes or until thickened. Transfer to an airtight container and refrigerate until cool. **MAKES 1¼ CUPS**

passionfruit chia jam

Place **1½ cups (180g) passionfruit pulp**, **¼ cup (55g) raw caster (superfine) sugar** and **¼ cup (60ml) water** in a non-stick frying pan over medium-high heat. Cook for 15 minutes or until the passionfruit has softened. Remove from the heat. Add **2 tablespoons white chia seeds** and stir to combine. Allow to stand for 30 minutes or until thickened. Transfer to an airtight container and refrigerate until cool. **MAKES 1¼ CUPS**

Instant

I'm all for fast fixes that return big on deliciousness.
When I can make an almost-instant dessert that features
an irresistibly gooey centre and nostalgia-soaked flavour
combination in as little as 10 minutes – everyone wins!

Puddings

chocolate mud pies

4 eggs
⅓ cup (80ml) light-flavoured extra virgin olive oil or
grapeseed oil
1 cup (150g) coconut sugar
⅔ cup (70g) cocoa
¾ cup (90g) almond meal (ground almonds)
2 teaspoons vanilla extract
vanilla bean ice-cream, to serve

TIP
For a pretty finish, choose an eco-friendly brown baking paper for these mud pies, so you don't miss a morsel!

Preheat oven to 160°C (325°F).

Place the eggs, oil, sugar, cocoa, almond meal and vanilla in a bowl and whisk to combine.

Pour into 4 x 1-cup (250ml) capacity ovenproof dishes lined with non-stick baking paper. Bake for 15 minutes or until just set.

Serve warm with ice-cream. **SERVES 4**

SCAN TO WATCH ME
CREATE THIS RECIPE

lemon chia cheesecake puddings

¼ cup (50g) white chia seeds
125g cream cheese, softened
2 cups (500g) plain thick yoghurt
2 teaspoons finely grated lemon rind
¼ cup (60ml) lemon juice
½ cup (125ml) light agave syrup
crushed blackberries
1 cup (125g) blackberries
2 teaspoons raw caster (superfine) sugar

TIP
These puddings soften over time, so eat them within 48 hours of making them.

Place the chia seeds in a blender and blend to a fine powder. Add the cream cheese, yoghurt, lemon rind, lemon juice and agave syrup and blend to combine.

Divide the mixture between serving glasses and refrigerate for 2 hours or until set.

To make the crushed blackberries, place the blackberries and sugar in a bowl and mix to combine. Lightly crush the blackberries.

Top each pudding with the crushed blackberries, to serve. **SERVES 4**

passionfruit pudding cups

½ cup (110g) raw caster (superfine) sugar
⅓ cup (40g) fresh passionfruit pulp
1 teaspoon finely grated lime rind
2 eggs
1⅓ cups (165g) almond meal (ground almonds)
1 teaspoon baking powder
1 teaspoon vanilla extract
vanilla bean yoghurt or ice-cream and extra passionfruit pulp,
  to serve

TIP
Try making
these with
fresh or frozen
berries – simply
swap the
passionfruit
pulp for ⅔ cup
of your
chosen berries.

Place the sugar, passionfruit, lime rind, eggs, almond meal, baking powder and vanilla in a bowl and whisk to combine.

Spoon the mixture into 4 x 1-cup (250ml) capacity microwave-safe and ovenproof mugs or ramekins.

To microwave the puddings, place the mugs in the microwave, one at a time, and cook on high for 1 minute 20 seconds or until the puddings are set around the edges and wobbly in the centre.

To bake the puddings, preheat oven to 160°C (325°F). Place the mugs on a baking tray and bake for 20–25 minutes or until the puddings are set around the edges and wobbly in the centre.

Serve with vanilla bean yoghurt and extra passionfruit pulp.

MAKES 4

instant banana pudding

½ cup (130g) mashed banana
1 tablespoon light-flavoured extra virgin olive oil
1 tablespoon coconut sugar
1 egg
1 teaspoon vanilla extract
¼ cup (40g) buckwheat flour
¼ teaspoon baking powder
¼ teaspoon ground cinnamon
chopped dark (70% cocoa) chocolate, extra ground cinnamon,
   blueberries and raw caster (superfine) sugar, for sprinkling

TIP
Don't be tempted to overcook this pudding – it should come out with a soft centre and will continue to cook as it stands.

Place the banana, oil, coconut sugar, egg and vanilla in a bowl and mix to combine. Add the buckwheat flour, baking powder and cinnamon and mix to combine.

Pour the mixture into a 1-cup (250ml) capacity microwave-safe mug or ramekin. Top with dark chocolate, extra cinnamon or blueberries and sugar.

Place in the microwave and cook on high for 1 minute 15 seconds or until the pudding is just set. Serve warm. **MAKES 1**

SCAN TO WATCH ME
CREATE THIS RECIPE

polenta cakes with orange blossom syrup

14 soft fresh dates (about 280g), pitted
5 eggs
⅓ cup (80ml) light-flavoured extra virgin olive oil
⅔ cup (120g) instant polenta
1 cup (120g) almond meal (ground almonds)
1 cup (220g) raw caster (superfine) sugar
2 tablespoons finely grated orange rind
1 teaspoon baking powder
1 teaspoon vanilla extract
orange blossom syrup
½ cup (125ml) fresh orange juice
¼ cup (90g) honey
2 teaspoons orange blossom water+
shredded rind of 1 orange

Preheat oven to 160°C (325°F). Grease a 12 x ⅓-cup (80ml) capacity muffin tin.

Place the dates, eggs, oil, polenta, almond meal, sugar, orange rind, baking powder and vanilla in a blender or food processor and blend until smooth.

Pour into the prepared tin and bake for 20–25 minutes or until cooked when tested with a skewer. Allow to cool slightly in the tin, before carefully turning out onto a wire rack.

Meanwhile, make the orange blossom syrup. Place the orange juice, honey, orange blossom water and rind in a small frying pan over medium heat. Bring to the boil and cook for 4–5 minutes or until slightly reduced and syrupy.

Pour the orange blossom syrup over the warm cakes, to serve.

MAKES 12

+ *Find orange blossom water at select supermarkets or specialty food stores.*

Flavoured Yoghurt

No ice-cream? No worries – a humble tub of yoghurt and some pantry staples are all you need to create creamy dollops of yum that will elevate sweet treats in a flash.

vanilla cinnamon yoghurt

Place **1½ cups (375g) plain thick yoghurt**, **1 tablespoon pure maple syrup** and **½ teaspoon ground cinnamon** in a bowl and mix to combine. Top with **2 teaspoons vanilla bean paste** and swirl through. MAKES 1½ CUPS

rose and raspberry yoghurt

Place ½ cup (60g) raspberries, 1 tablespoon honey and 1 teaspoon rosewater in a bowl and lightly crush to combine. Add 1½ cups (375g) plain thick yoghurt and mix to combine. Sprinkle with edible rose petals, if desired. MAKES 2 CUPS

lemon and vanilla yoghurt

Place 1½ cups (375g) plain thick yoghurt, 1 tablespoon light agave syrup, 2 teaspoons vanilla extract and 2 teaspoons finely grated lemon rind in a bowl and mix to combine. Sprinkle with extra finely grated lemon rind, if desired. MAKES 1½ CUPS

caramel yoghurt

Place 1½ cups (375g) plain thick yoghurt in a bowl and top with 1½ tablespoons coconut sugar. Allow to stand for 1–2 minutes, then swirl through. MAKES 1½ CUPS

Glossary + Index

agave syrup

Agave syrup is the nectar of the succulent and has a mild, neutral sweetness. It's often used in place of sugar, maple syrup or honey. It's available from the health food aisle of supermarkets as light or dark agave. Light agave syrup is used in this book for its milder flavour.

almond butter

This paste is made from ground almonds and is available at most supermarkets and health food stores. It's a popular alternative to peanut butter for those with peanut allergies (always check the label). Sometimes sold as 'spreads', the nut butters called for in this book are all-natural with no additives.

almond meal (ground almonds)

Almond meal is available from most supermarkets. Take care not to confuse it with almond flour, which has a much finer texture. Make your own almond meal by processing whole almonds to a meal in a food processor – 125g (4½ oz) almonds should give 1 cup of almond meal.

baking powder

A raising agent used in baking, consisting of bicarbonate of soda and/or cream of tartar. Most are gluten free (check the label). Baking powder that's kept beyond its use-by date can lose effectiveness.

beans

black beans

Popular in Latin American cuisine, these small shiny beans have a dense, meaty texture and are commonly used in Mexican dishes and salads. Available canned (tinned) at most supermarkets.

white beans (cannellini beans)

Also known as cannellini beans, these large white kidney-shaped beans are packed full of protein and fibre and used in soups, stews and salads, or to add flavour and body to patties and meatballs.

blanching

Blanching is a cooking method used to slightly soften the texture, heighten the colour and enhance the flavour of vegetables. Plunge the ingredient briefly into boiling unsalted water, remove and refresh under cold water. Drain well.

bok choy

A mild-flavoured green vegetable, with fresh crunchy white stems and broad floppy green leaves. It's also known as Chinese chard, Chinese white cabbage or pak choy. Best trimmed, gently steamed, pan-fried or blanched, then teamed with Asian-style rice and noodle dishes or stir-fries.

broccolini (sprouting broccoli)

Also known as tenderstem broccoli, broccolini is a cross between gai lan (Chinese broccoli) and broccoli. This popular green vegetable has long, thin stems and small florets with a slightly sweet flavour. Sold in bunches, broccolini can be substituted with regular heads of broccoli that have been sliced into slim florets.

butter

Unless it says otherwise in a recipe, butter should be at room temperature for cooking. It should not be half-melted or too soft to handle. We mostly prefer unsalted butter, but use salted if you wish.

buttermilk

Despite its name, buttermilk contains no butter. It has a light, creamy and slightly tangy flavour, which makes it a healthier creamy addition to pasta sauces and soups. It contains cultures and acids that react with raising agents to produce carbon dioxide, which creates light and fluffy cakes, scones and pancakes.

cabbage

green

Pale green or white with tightly bound, waxy leaves, these common cabbages are sold whole or halved in supermarkets and are perfect for use in slaws. Choose heads that are firm and unblemished with crisp leaves that are tightly packed.

wombok (Chinese)

Also known as napa cabbage or Chinese cabbage, wombok is elongated in shape with ribbed green-yellow leaves. It's regularly used in noodle salads and to make kimchi. Find it at most supermarkets.

capers

These small green flower buds of the caper bush are packed either in brine or salt. Capers lend their salty-sour intensity to sauces, seafood and pastas. Before using, rinse thoroughly, drain and pat dry.

cashew butter

This paste is made from ground cashews and is available at most supermarkets and health food stores. Often sold as 'spreads', the nut butters called for in this book are all-natural with no additives. Popular in baking recipes, cashew butter often gives cookies and slices a fudgy texture.

cheese

blue
The distinctive blue veins and strong flavour of blue cheeses are achieved by adding a cultured mould. Most have a soft-yet-crumbly texture and acidic taste, which becomes rounded and more mellow with age. Blue cheeses team particularly well with sweet flavours – they're often paired on cheese boards and in salads with quince paste, pear, honey or figs.

buffalo mozzarella
This much-loved variety of fresh Italian mozzarella is made from water buffalo's milk and/or cow's milk. Creamy and salty, it's sold in rounds, or balls, at grocers and delicatessens and is often torn into pieces and scattered over caprese salads, pizza or pasta.

burrata
An Italian stretched-curd cheese made from mozzarella, with a creamy, milky centre. It's best served simply, with something like a tomato or fig salad. It's available from most supermarkets or delis.

feta
A brined white cheese typically bought in blocks that is Greek in origin, feta has a salty, tangy flavour ranging from mild to sharp. Traditionally made using sheep's milk, these days you can find many cow's milk versions. Use it fresh in salads, as a salty hit of creaminess over vegies, or baked.

haloumi
A firm white Cypriot cheese made from sheep's milk, haloumi has a stringy texture and is usually sold in brine. Slice and pan-fry until golden and heated through for a salty addition to roast vegetables or salads. Buy haloumi at major greengrocers and supermarkets.

marinated feta
Feta that is preserved in a mix of olive oil, herbs and other flavours. Use crumbled over salads, roast vegetables or toast. Available from most supermarkets or delis.

parmesan
Italy's favourite hard, granular cheese is made from cow's milk. Parmigiano Reggiano is the best variety, made under strict guidelines in the Emilia-Romagna region and aged for an average of two years. Grana Padano mainly comes from Lombardy and is aged for around 15 months.

ricotta
A creamy, finely grained white cheese. Ricotta means 'recooked' in Italian, a reference to the way the cheese is produced by heating the whey leftover from making other cheese varieties. It's fresh, creamy and low in fat and there is also a reduced-fat version, which is lighter again. Choose fresh ricotta from your delicatessen or supermarket deli.

chia seeds
These ancient seeds come from a flowering plant and are full of protein, omega-3 fatty acids, minerals and fibre. Use the black or white seeds interchangeably. Find them in supermarkets – they're great for smoothies, salads and baking.

chickpeas (garbanzo beans)
A legume native to western Asia and across the Mediterranean, chickpeas are used in soups, stews and are the base ingredient in hummus. Dried chickpeas need soaking before use; buy them canned to skip this step.

chillies
There are more than 200 different types of chillies, or chilli peppers, in the world. Long red or green chillies are generally milder, fruitier and sweeter, while small chillies are much hotter. Remove the membranes and seeds for a milder result.

chipotle in adobo sauce
Chipotle are smoke-dried jalapeño chillies. In adobo sauce, they're sold in cans or jars at supermarkets, specialty grocers and delicatessens. They are popular in Mexican cuisine and also add a great kick when stirred through mayonnaise, in tacos or tortillas, or to add punchy flavour to patties, meat dishes, or anywhere you would add chillies.

jalapeños
These dark green plump Mexican chillies are known for their medium heat and fresh, bitey flavour. Buy jalapeños sliced in jars, pickled or fresh. Often used in Mexican cuisine, like in tacos or to give salsas a fiery edge, much of their heat is held in the seeds and membranes, which can be removed if you prefer a milder intensity.

Chinese cooking wine (Shaoxing)
Similar to dry sherry, Shaoxing, or Chinese cooking wine, is a blend of glutinous rice, millet, a special yeast and the local spring waters of Shaoxing in northern China, where it is traditionally made. Used in myriad sauces and dressings, it's available from the Asian section of supermarkets and at Asian grocers.

chorizo

Originating in Spain, this fermented, cured and spiced pork sausage imparts a smoky, meaty flavour to dishes. Mexican chorizo is often made using fresh pork while Spanish varieties use smoked pork and feature pimenton (Spanish paprika).

coconut

coconut aminos

Made from the sap of coconut flowers, coconut aminos is a vegan and soy-free alternative to soy sauce and fish sauce. Find it in the Asian aisle of select supermarkets or at Asian grocers.

cream

The cream that rises to the top after the first pressing of coconut milk, coconut cream is higher both in energy and fat than regular coconut milk. It's a common ingredient in curries and Asian sweets. You can buy cocout cream in cans or cartons from most supermarkets.

desiccated

Desiccated coconut is coconut meat that has been shredded and dried to remove its moisture. It's unsweetened and very powdery. Great for baking as well as savoury Asian sauces and sambals.

flakes

Coconut flakes have a large shape and chewier texture than the desiccated variety, and are often used for decorating and in mueslis and baking. Buy them ready-toasted, with lovely golden edges, from supermarkets.

coconut milk

A milky, sweet liquid made by soaking grated fresh coconut flesh or desiccated coconut in warm water and squeezing it through muslin or cheesecloth. Coconut milk shouldn't be confused with coconut water, which is a clear liquid found inside young coconuts.

sugar

See *sugar (coconut)*, page 260.

coriander (cilantro)

This pungent green herb is common in Asian and Mexican cooking. The finely chopped roots are sometimes incorporated into curry pastes. The dried seeds can't be substituted for fresh coriander.

crème fraîche

A rich, tangy, fermented cream, traditionally from France, with a minimum fat content of 35 per cent. Available at grocers, delicatessens and most supermarkets.

curry paste

The store-bought curry pastes called for in this book are Thai-style. Whether red or green, choose a good-quality paste for superior results. Available from the Asian aisle of most supermarkets.

dark chocolate

The dark chocolate called for in this book is 70% cocoa solids. Chocolate that has 70% cocoa solids is usually labelled as such, and has a more bitter, intense flavour and no powdery texture. It's sold in blocks and is ideal for use in baking. Find it in the baking aisle of supermarkets.

dates

With their smooth, sticky texture and deep caramel flavour, Medjool dates, referred to in this book as soft fresh dates, are called for in baked and raw treats. Not to be confused with dried dates, which have undergone a heating process.

dukkah

A Middle-Eastern nut and spice blend available from select supermarkets, spice shops and specialty grocers, widely used sprinkled over meats and salads, or used in a spice crust. It often contains sesame seeds, herbs, nuts and spice.

edamame

Find these tasty, tender soy beans ready-podded in the freezer section of major greengrocers, Asian grocers and some supermarkets. They are a great addition to salads, stir-fries and pastas, or used like you would other legumes in patties.

eggs

The standard egg size used in this book is 60g (2 oz). It's important to use the right sized eggs, for baking recipes especially, as it can affect the outcome. Room temperature eggs are best for baking.

fish sauce

This amber-coloured liquid drained from salted, fermented fish is used to add flavour to Thai, Vietnamese or Southeast Asian dishes, such as curries, noodles or salads, plus dressings and dipping sauces.

flaxseeds (linseeds)

These small brown seeds have a nutty flavour and are high in omega-3. They can be baked into bread, sprinkled in muesli and salads or used to make slices. Find them at supermarkets or health food stores.

flour

buckwheat

Despite its name, buckwheat flour isn't from a grain but is milled from the seed of a plant related to rhubarb and sorrel. Often used in pancakes and noodles for its rich, nutty flavour and wholesome benefits, it's also a gluten free flour substitute in cakes.

cornflour (cornstarch)

When made from ground corn or maize, cornflour is gluten free. Recipes often require it to be blended with water or stock for use as a thickening agent. Not to be confused with cornflour in the United States, which is actually finely ground corn meal.

plain (all-purpose)

Ground from the endosperm of wheat, plain white flour contains no raising agent and is the most commonly used flour.

rice

Rice flour is a fine flour made from ground rice. Available in white and brown varieties, it's often used as a thickening agent in baking, in cookies and shortbreads, and to coat foods when cooking Asian dishes. It's gluten free and available in supermarkets and health food stores. Not to be confused with rice starch.

wholemeal (whole-wheat)

Ground from the whole grain of wheat and thus keeping more of its nutrients and fibre, this flour is available in plain (all-purpose) and self-raising (self-rising) varieties from most supermarkets and health food stores.

farro

Farro is an ancient variety of wheat that is sold dry and is cooked in water. Its firm, chewy texture and light, nutty flavour make it a great addition to salads, risottos and soups. Farro can be found in supermarkets and health food stores. 1 cup cooked farro weighs 200g (7 oz). Directions for cooking farro are as follows.

1 cup (200g) farro
2½ cups (625ml) water
pinch of salt

Place the farro, water and salt in a medium saucepan over high heat. Bring to the boil, cover with a tight-fitting lid and reduce heat to medium-low. Cook for 15–20 minutes or until tender. Drain any remaining water. **MAKES 2½ CUPS (450G)**

freekeh

Freekeh is the immature or 'green' wheat grain that has been roasted. The recipes in this book call for whole-grain freekeh as opposed to cracked freekeh. The grains can be used in salads and tabouli or eat it as you would rice or pasta. Find it in supermarkets and health food stores. 1 cup cooked freekeh weighs 160g (5½ oz). Directions for cooking freekeh are as follows.

1 cup (220g) freekeh
3 cups (750ml) water

Place the freekeh and water in a medium saucepan over high heat. Bring to the boil, immediately cover with a tight-fitting lid and reduce the heat to low. Cook for 30–35 minutes or until tender. Drain any remaining water. **MAKES 3 CUPS (480G)**

gai lan (Chinese broccoli)

Also known as Chinese broccoli or Chinese kale, gai lan is a leafy vegetable with dark green leaves, tiny white or yellow flowers and stout stems.

garam masala

A blend of cumin and allspice, garam masala is found in the spice aisle of most supermarkets and widely used in Indian and Middle-Eastern cooking.

gochujang

This is a spicy, savoury and slightly sweet red chilli paste originating in Korea, made from fermented rice, wheat and red chillies. Find it in the Asian section of the supermarket or in Asian supermarkets.

green onions (scallions)

Both the white and green part of these long mild onions are used in salads, as a garnish and in Asian cooking. Sold in bunches, they give a fresh bite to dishes. Find them at the supermarket, Asian supermarkets or greengrocers.

harissa

A northern African red chilli paste made from chilli, garlic and spices including coriander, caraway and cumin. Available in jars and tubes from select supermarkets and specialty stores. If you can't find it, use another mild-to-medium red chilli paste.

hoisin sauce

This thick, sweet and salty sauce is used extensively in Chinese cuisine. It is a dark soy-based sauce that can be used as a glaze, in sauces and as a dipping sauce. Find it in the Asian aisle in the supermarket.

kecap manis
Also known as sweet soy sauce, kecap manis or ketjap manis is a type of soy sauce that originated in Indonesia. It is thicker and sweeter than soy sauce. Find it in the Asian food section of most supermarkets.

labne
Find this creamy, strained, Middle-Eastern yoghurt cheese in tubs in the chilled section of greengrocers, gourmet food stores and some supermarkets.

Lebanese cucumber
This sweet-flavoured, crisp-fleshed and smooth-skinned cucumber is featured throughout this book, and is used widely in salads. It is similar to the English cucumber, Persian cucumber and the American garden cucumber.

lemongrass
A tall lemon-scented grass used in Asian cooking. Peel away the outer leaves and chop the tender white root-end finely, or add in large pieces during cooking and remove before serving. If adding in larger pieces, bruise them with the back of a kitchen knife. Often used in curry pastes for its fragrant flavour profile. Find it at supermarkets and grocers.

maple syrup
A sweetener made from the sap of the maple tree, be sure to use pure maple syrup. Imitation, or pancake, syrup is made from corn syrup flavoured with maple and does not have the same intensity of flavour. The maple syrup referred to throughout this book is pure maple syrup, free from additives and preservatives.

mirin (Japanese rice wine)
Mirin is a pale yellow, sweet and tangy Japanese cooking wine made from glutinous rice and alcohol.

miso paste
Miso is a traditional Japanese ingredient produced by fermenting rice, barley or soy beans to a paste. It's used for sauces and spreads, pickling vegetables, and is often mixed with dashi stock to serve as miso soup. Sometimes labelled simply 'miso', white, yellow and red varieties are available, their flavour increasing in intensity with their colour. The recipes in this book call for white (shiro) miso for its delicate flavour and colour. Find miso paste in supermarkets and Asian grocers.

noodles
Most fresh noodles will keep in the fridge for up to a week. Keep a supply of dried noodles in the pantry for last-minute meals. Available from supermarkets and Asian food stores.

dried rice
Fine, dried (stick) noodles common in southeast Asian cooking. Depending on their thickness, rice noodles need only be boiled briefly, or soaked in hot water until soft.

fresh egg
Made from wheat flour, water and egg, these springy, chewy noodles are sold fresh in the fridge section of supermarkets or Asian grocers.

rice vermicelli
Very thin dried rice noodles sometimes called rice sticks. They are usually used in soups such as laksa, in rice paper rolls and in salads.

soba
Japanese noodles made from buckwheat and wheat flour, soba are greyish brown in colour and served in cold salads or in hot soups.

oil
extra virgin olive
Graded according to its flavour, aroma and acidity. Extra virgin is the highest-quality olive oil; it contains no more than 1% acid. Virgin is the next best; it contains 1.5% or less acid. Bottles labelled simply 'olive oil' contain a blend of refined and unrefined virgin olive oil. 'Light' olive oil is the least pure in quality and shouldn't be confused with light-flavoured extra virgin olive oil.

grapeseed
A by-product of winemaking, grapeseed oil is made using the pressed seeds of grapes. It has a surprisingly neutral flavour. Choose grapeseed oil that has been cold-pressed. Find it at most supermarkets.

light-flavoured extra virgin olive
This is still the highest-quality olive oil and is made from a pure blend of the oil from milder-flavoured olives.

sesame
Pressed from sesame seeds, sesame oil is used in Asian cuisine more as a nutty, full-flavoured seasoning than a cooking medium.

panko
These breadcrumbs have a drier, flakier texture than regular breadcrumbs. Widely used in Japanese cuisine and to produce crumbs for proteins and vegetables.

paprika, smoked

Unlike Hungarian paprika, the Spanish style, known as pimentón, is deep and smoky. It is made from smoked, ground pimento peppers and comes in varying intensities, from sweet and mild (dulce), bittersweet medium hot (agridulce) and hot (picante). The variety called for in this book is smoky.

peanut butter

Made from ground dry-roasted peanuts, the peanut butter referred to in this book is all-natural and free from additives, sweeteners or emulsifiers. It's sold in crunchy or smooth varieties in supermarkets and used in this book to give a nutty, creamy kick to curries and noodles.

pepitas (pumpkin seeds)

Pumpkin seeds are hulled to reveal these olive green kernels that, once dried, are nutty in flavour and easy to use in smoothies, baking and salads. Find them in supermarkets.

pickled ginger

Also known as gari, this Japanese condiment is made from young ginger that's been pickled in sugar and vinegar. It's commonly served with Japanese food as a palate cleanser, but is becoming popular as a tangy addition to sushi bowls and salads. Buy it in jars from Asian grocers and some supermarkets.

pita bread

A yeast-leavened round flatbread made from wheat flour and common in Mediterranean and Middle Eastern cuisine, and neighbouring regions. Often served lightly toasted to wrap up meat and vegies and is sold at select supermarkets and delis.

pomegranate molasses

A concentrated syrup made from pomegranate juice, with a sweet, tart flavour, pomegranate molasses is available from Middle Eastern grocery stores and specialty food shops. If you can't find it, try using caramelised balsamic vinegar.

pomegranate seeds

The small pink seeds from inside the pomegranate, featuring a sweet and slightly tart flavour. Commonly used in desserts or salads. To extract the seeds, cut the pomegranate in half, hold it over a bowl and, using a wooden spoon, smack the skin firmly until the seeds pop out.

quinoa

Packed with protein, this grain-like seed has a chewy texture, nutty flavour and is fluffy when cooked. Use it as you would couscous or rice. It freezes well, so any excess cooked quinoa can be frozen in individual portions. Red and black varieties, which require a slightly longer cooking time, are also available in most supermarkets. 1 cup cooked white quinoa weighs 160g (5½ oz). Directions for cooking quinoa are as follows.

1 cup (180g) white quinoa
1¼ cups (310ml) water
sea salt flakes

Place the quinoa, water and a pinch of salt in a medium saucepan over high heat. Bring to the boil, cover immediately with a tight-fitting lid and reduce the heat to low. Simmer for 12 minutes or until almost tender. Remove from the heat and allow to steam for 8 minutes or until tender.
MAKES 2¾ CUPS (440G)

black/red

Black or red varieties of quinoa are available at most supermarkets. Mostly selected for their colour, they can vary from regular quinoa in texture when cooked, but all three are essentially interchangeable.

flakes

Quinoa flakes are simply quinoa seeds that have been steam-rolled into flakes. Use them in muesli or baked goods, or as a healthier crumb coating for proteins. Find them at most supermarkets.

rice
basmati

A type of long-grain aromatic white rice that retains its long slender length when cooked and contains higher levels of protein than regular white rice. Available at supermarkets.

brown

Brown rice is different to white rice in that the bran and germ of the wholegrain are intact. This renders it nutritionally superior and gives it a nutty chewiness. It's available at supermarkets. 1 cup cooked brown rice weighs 200g (7 oz). Directions for cooking brown rice are as follows.

1 cup (200g) brown rice
1½ cups (375ml) water
sea salt flakes

Place the rice, water and a pinch of salt in a medium saucepan over high heat. Bring to the boil, immediately cover with a tight-fitting lid and reduce the heat to low. Simmer for 25 minutes or until almost tender. Remove from the heat and allow to steam for 10 minutes or until tender. **MAKES 2 CUPS (400G)**

black
Also known as purple rice, this rice, popular in Japanese cuisine, gets its signature colour from a pigment called anthocyanin. Once cooked, it has a chewy texture similar to brown rice. Available at select supermarkets and specialty stores.

jasmine
A long-grain white rice popular for its shape-holding, slender grains and fragrant scent. Available at most supermarkets.

rice flour
See *flours (rice)*, page 257.

sage
This Mediterranean herb has a distinct, fragrant flavour and soft, oval-shaped grey-green leaves. It's used often in Italian cooking, crisped in a pan with butter or oil.

sesame seeds
These small seeds have a nutty flavour and can be used in savoury and sweet cooking. White sesame seeds are the most common variety, but black, or unhulled, seeds are popular for coatings in Asian cooking.

shiso leaves
Sometimes called perilla, this herb comes in both green and purple-leafed varieties. It has a slight peppery flavour and is often used to wrap ingredients. The micro variety makes a pretty garnish. Find it at some greengrocers and Asian markets.

Sichuan peppercorns
Sometimes called Szechuan pepper or Chinese prickly ash, this Chinese pepper is commonly used in Sichuan cuisine. They offer an intense, numbing, tingling spiciness, which mellows a little when the pepper is toasted and crushed. Sichuan peppers offer a deep spicy flavour to Asian dishes such as noodles and stir-fries. Find them at Asian grocers.

sorrel leaves
This leafy green has a signature sour flavour. The red-veined leaves are a pretty and nutritious addition to salads or as a leafy garnish. Find red-veined sorrel leaves at your local greengrocer.

sourdough bread
A naturally leavened bread that uses a 'starter' – a fermented flour and water mixture that contains wild yeast and good bacteria – to rise, giving it a slightly chewy texture and a tangy flavour. Sourdough is also often free from additives. It's used widely in this book to make breadcrumbs for its sturdiness, or for making crunchy croutons.

sugar
Extracted as crystals from the juice of the sugar cane plant, sugar is a sweetener, flavour enhancer and food preservative.

brown
In Australia, what is known as 'brown sugar' is referred to as 'light brown sugar' in other parts of the world. Light and dark brown sugars are made from refined sugar with natural molasses added. Light and dark types are interchangeable if either is unavailable. An important ingredient in cookies, puddings, dense cakes and brownies, you can find both varieties of brown sugar in supermarkets.

caster (superfine)
The superfine granule of caster sugar gives baked products a light texture and crumb, which is important for many cakes and delicate desserts. Caster sugar is essential for making meringue, as the fine crystals dissolve more easily in the whipped eggwhite.

coconut
With an earthy, butterscotch flavour, coconut sugar, or coconut palm sugar, comes from the flowers of the coconut palm. Coconut sugar gives a lovely depth of flavour. Find it in select supermarkets, and at Asian grocers.

demerara
Demerara is a coarse-grained golden cane sugar, with a mild molasses flavour. Like raw sugar, it is delicious when stirred into coffee or sprinkled over baked treats for a sweet caramel crust.

icing (confectioner's)
Icing sugar is granulated sugar ground to a very fine powder. When mixed with liquid or into butter or cream cheese, it creates a sweet glaze or icing, plus it can be sifted over cakes or desserts. Unless specified, use pure icing sugar, not icing sugar mixture, which contains cornflour (cornstarch) and needs more liquid.

raw (golden) caster
Light brown in colour and honey-like in flavour, raw sugar is slightly less refined than white sugar, with a larger granule. It lends a more pronounced flavour and colour to baked goods. You can use demerara sugar in its place.

sumac

These dried berries of a flowering plant are ground to produce an acidic, vibrant crimson powder that's popular in the Middle East. Sumac has a lemony flavour and is great sprinkled on salads, dips, yoghurt or chicken. Find it at supermarkets and specialty spice shops.

sunflower seeds

These small grey kernels from the black and white seeds of sunflowers are mostly processed for their oil. The kernels are also found in snack mixes and muesli, and can be baked into breads and slices. Buy sunflower seeds in supermarkets.

tahini

A thick paste made from ground sesame seeds, tahini is widely used in Middle-Eastern cooking. It's available in jars and cans from supermarkets and health food stores, in both hulled and unhulled varieties. The recipes in this book call for hulled tahini, for its slightly smoother texture.

tempeh

A plant-based food made from fermented soybeans, tempeh is rich in protein. It's similar to tofu but with a heartier, chewier texture and nuttier flavour. Use it like you would tofu. Find it at most supermarkets.

Thai lime leaves

Also known as kaffir or makrut lime, these fragrant leaves have a distinctive double-leaf structure. Commonly crushed or shredded and used as a garnish, the leaves are available fresh or dried, from most greengrocers and at Asian food stores. Fresh leaves are more flavourful and freeze well.

tofu

Not all tofu is created equal. The recipes in this book call for either firm or silken tofu, which can be found in the chilled section of the supermarket. Where possible, choose organic non-GMO tofu. All brands vary in texture and taste, so don't give up until you find one you love. It's a great source of protein and acts like a sponge for flavour.

tortilla

A thin, unleavened, round flatbread that is a popular vessel for tacos, quesadillas and other Mexican dishes, as well as for wraps. Traditionally made from corn flour, nowadays, wheat flour is often used to make flour tortillas.

vanilla

bean paste

This store-bought paste is a convenient way to replace whole vanilla beans and is great in desserts. One teaspoon of paste substitutes for one vanilla bean.

beans

These fragrant cured pods from the vanilla orchid are used whole, often split and the tiny seeds inside scraped into the mixture to infuse flavour into cream-based recipes.

extract

For a pure vanilla taste, use a good-quality vanilla extract, not an essence or imitation flavour. Vanilla extract features a rounded, rich vanilla flavour.

vinegar

apple cider

Made from apple must, apple cider vinegar has a golden amber colour and a sour appley flavour. Use it to make dressings, marinades and chutneys. The recipes in this book call for organic or unfiltered apple cider vinegar.

balsamic

Originally from Modena in Italy, there are many balsamics on the market ranging in quality and flavour. Aged varieties are preferable. A milder white version is also available, which is used where colour is important. Find it at supermarkets or specialty stores.

malt vinegar

Made from malted grains of barley, malt vinegar is used for its tart flavour as a dipping sauce or finishing vinegar over hot foods.

rice wine

Made from fermenting rice (or rice wine), rice wine vinegar is milder and sweeter than vinegars that are made by oxidising distilled wine or other alcohol made from grapes. Rice wine vinegar is available in white, black, brown and red varieties and can be found in supermarkets and Asian food stores.

wine

Both red and white wine can be distilled into vinegar. Use in dressings, glazes and preserved condiments such as pickles. Use it to make a classic French vinaigrette.

yoghurt, natural Greek-style

Recipes in this book call for natural, unsweetened full-fat Greek-style (thick) yoghurt. Buy it from the chilled aisle of the supermarket, checking the label for any unwanted sweeteners or artificial flavours.

global measures

Measures vary from Europe to the US and even from Australia to New Zealand.

metric and imperial

Measuring cups and spoons may vary slightly from one country to another, but the difference is generally not sufficient to affect a recipe. The recipes in this book use Australian measures. All cup and spoon measures are level. An Australian measuring cup holds 250ml (8½ fl oz).

One Australian metric teaspoon holds 5ml (⅛ fl oz), one Australian tablespoon holds 20ml (¾ fl oz) (4 teaspoons). However, in the USA, New Zealand and the UK, 15ml (½ fl oz) (3-teaspoon) tablespoons are used.

When measuring dry ingredients, add the ingredient loosely to the cup and level with a knife. Don't tap or shake to compact the ingredient unless the recipe requests 'firmly packed'.

liquids and solids

Measuring cups, spoons and scales are great assets in the kitchen – these equivalents are a guide.

liquids

cup	metric	imperial
⅛ cup	30ml	1 fl oz
¼ cup	60ml	2 fl oz
⅓ cup	80ml	2¾ fl oz
½ cup	125ml	4¼ fl oz
⅔ cup	160ml	5½ fl oz
¾ cup	180ml	6 fl oz
1 cup	250ml	8½ fl oz
2 cups	500ml	17 fl oz
3 cups	750ml	25 fl oz
4 cups	1 litre	34 fl oz

solids

metric	imperial
20g	¾ oz
60g	2 oz
125g	4½ oz
180g	6¼ oz
250g	8¾ oz
450g	1 lb
750g	1 lb 10 oz
1kg	2 lb 3 oz

more equivalents

Here are a few more simplified equivalents for metric and imperial measures, plus ingredient names.

millimetres to inches

metric	imperial
3mm	⅛ inch
6mm	¼ inch
1cm	½ inch
2.5cm	1 inch
5cm	2 inches
18cm	7 inches
20cm	8 inches
23cm	9 inches
25cm	10 inches
30cm	12 inches

ingredient equivalents

almond meal	ground almonds
bicarbonate of soda	baking soda
caster sugar	superfine sugar
celeriac	celery root
chickpeas	garbanzo beans
coriander	cilantro
cornflour	cornstarch
cos lettuce	romaine lettuce
eggplant	aubergine
gai lan	chinese broccoli
green onion	scallion
icing sugar	confectioner's sugar
plain flour	all-purpose flour
rocket	arugula
self-raising flour	self-rising flour
silverbeet	swiss chard
snow pea	mange tout
white sugar	granulated sugar
zucchini	courgette

oven temperatures

Setting the oven to the correct
temperature can be crucial
when baking sweet things.

celsius to fahrenheit

celsius	fahrenheit
100°C	200°F
120°C	250°F
140°C	275°F
150°C	300°F
160°C	325°F
180°C	350°F
190°C	375°F
200°C	400°F
220°C	425°F

electric to gas

celsius	gas
110°C	¼
130°C	½
140°C	1
150°C	2
170°C	3
180°C	4
190°C	5
200°C	6
220°C	7
230°C	8
240°C	9
250°C	10

butter and eggs

Let 'fresh is best' be your
mantra when it comes to
selecting eggs and dairy goods.

butter

We generally use unsalted butter
as it allows for a little more
control over a recipe's flavour.
Either way, the impact is minimal.
Salted butter has a longer
shelf life and is preferred by
some people. One American
stick of butter is 125g (4½ oz).
One Australian block of butter
is 250g (8¾ oz).

eggs

Unless otherwise indicated,
we use large (60g/2 oz) chicken
eggs. To preserve freshness, store
eggs in the refrigerator in the
carton they are sold in. Use only
the freshest eggs in recipes such
as mayonnaise or dressings that
use raw or barely cooked eggs.
Be extra cautious if there is
a salmonella problem in your
community, particularly in food
that is to be served to children,
pregnant women or the elderly.

useful weights

Here are a few simple weight
conversions for cupfuls of
commonly used ingredients.

common ingredients

almond meal (ground almonds)
1 cup | 120g | 4¼ oz
brown sugar
1 cup | 240g | 8½ oz
raw caster (superfine) sugar
1 cup | 220g | 7¾ oz
coconut sugar
1 cup | 150g | 5¼ oz
desiccated coconut
1 cup | 80g | 2¾ oz
**plain (all-purpose)
or self-raising (self-rising) flour**
1 cup | 150g | 5¼ oz
fresh sourdough breadcrumbs
1 cup | 70g | 2½ oz
raw or roasted cashews
1 cup | 150g | 5¼ oz
plain thick yoghurt
1 cup | 250g | 9 oz
uncooked brown rice
1 cup | 200g | 7 oz
cooked brown rice
1 cup | 165g | 5¾ oz
cooked quinoa
1 cup | 140g | 5 oz
fresh or frozen berries
1 cup | 125g | 4½ oz

thank you

Not a day goes by that I am not grateful for the talented people I get to surround myself with – to create with, laugh with, and taste and style recipes alongside.

My creative director Chi Lam, the always beautifully considered designer. Thank you for your zen, your seemingly effortless design wizardry and your problem-solving prowess.

It's hard to sum up all that you bring to the fold, Hannah Schubert. Your excellent managing editor and time-keeping skills, sharp design eye, barista talents and ability to think for me before I even knew I needed to think, are just some of your hidden talents!

To Chris Court, talented photographer, super studio DJ and handiest handy man. Thank you for these stunning images, for your solid snacking game and for always making me laugh.

To the always supportive Con Poulos, your beautiful images have shone through yet again. Thank you for always being up for trying something new and for your worldly and hilarious chats.

To Mariam Digges, my knowledgeable editor and all things words-crafter. Thank you for whipping my book into shape. I love that you have cooked so many of the recipes before the book even prints!

In the kitchen, thank you to Tina McLeish, aka passionate eco warrior, gardener and baking princess; and Jacinta Cannataci – your electric energy is always infectious! Thank you for helping bring my recipes to life.

To my thesaurus, continuity manager and script writer, Lauren Gibb. I'm grateful to have you in my corner.

At HarperCollinsPublishers, I must thank Catherine Milne, Jim Demetriou, Janelle Garside, Belinda Yuille and Sarah Haines. Without your continued support, none of this would be possible.

Thanks to my loyal partners Farmers Union, Glad to be Green® and Miele – it's been a pleasure to work with you. To ceramicists Marjoke De Heer (@marjokedeheer) and Angela Nicholson (@angela_nicholson_studio) – a heartfelt thank you for your stunning wares. At Hale Imports, thanks to Ross and Dan for my beautiful knives (@shun.australia).

Between writing and filming, my wonderful family and friends continue to cheer me on. Thank you for your unwavering love, support, and for always backing me up.

About Donna

As Australia's *leading food editor* and *best-selling cookbook author*, Donna Hay has made her way into the hearts (*and countless homes*) across the globe.

An *international publishing phenomenon*, Donna's name is synonymous with accessible yet *inspirational recipes* and *stunning images*. Her acclaimed magazine notched up an *incredible 100 issues* and her best-selling cookbooks have sold more than *eight million copies* worldwide.

The *donna hay brand* goes beyond the printed page, featuring an *impressive digital presence*; a number of *television series* (her latest is streaming on Disney+ in late 2022); branded merchandise; and a *baking mix range*. Donna adores living near the ocean with her two teenage boys and *still loves cooking* every single day.

Connect with Donna anytime, anywhere ...

www.donnahay.com   @donna.hay   pinterest.com/
donnahayhome

facebook.com/
donnahay